PREACHING ON
GOD'S JUSTICE

MOWBRAY PREACHING SERIES

Series Editor: D. W. Cleverley Ford

Preaching the Risen Christ: D. W. Cleverley Ford
Preaching on Devotional Occasions: D. W. Cleverley Ford
More Preaching on Favourite Hymns: Frank Colquhoun
Preaching on Special Occasions, Volume 3: Edward H. Patey
Preaching on Great Themes: D. W. Cleverley Ford
Preaching the Incarnate Christ: D. W. Cleverley Ford
Preaching for Our Planet: Hugh Montefiore
Preaching on the Crucifixion: D. W. Cleverley Ford
Preaching for All Seasons: John Vipond
Preaching on the Historical Jesus: D. W. Cleverley Ford
Preaching on God's Justice: John B. Taylor

Preaching at the Parish Communion:
ASB Epistles – Sundays: Year One, Volume 2: Dennis Runcorn
ASB Gospels – Sundays: Year Two, Volume 2: Peter Morris

PREACHING ON GOD'S JUSTICE

JOHN B. TAYLOR

MOWBRAY

Mowbray
A Cassell imprint
Villiers House
41/47 Strand
London
WC2N 5JE

First published 1994

British Library Cataloguing-in-Publication Data
A catalogue entry for this book is available from the British Library.

ISBN 0-264-67338-7

Printed and bound in Great Britain by Biddles Ltd, Guildford and King's Lynn

CONTENTS

Introduction   *page* vii

 1 The God of justice   1
 2 The ups and downs of life   7
 3 Safe havens   12
 4 An end to poverty   17
 5 'And a good judge too. . .'   21
 6 An eye for an eye   26
 7 What to do with refugees   30
 8 A bit of a fiddle   35
 9 Appearances are deceptive   40
10 Found out   44
11 The wisdom of Solomon   49
12 Compulsory purchase   54
13 Sunday trading   59
14 Right with God   64
15 Social evils   69
16 Off with the yoke   74
17 No justice   79
18 Drop the dead donkey   84
19 A long way from home   89
20 Mr Righteous   95
21 No back gates   100
22 Living in luxury   105
23 Shepherds or butchers   110
24 Who can stand?   115

INTRODUCTION

When the Series Editor kindly suggested to me that I write a sequel to my *Preaching through the Prophets*, it never occurred to me to do other than a further series of sermons on the Old Testament. This has been my love ever since my student days when I began to learn Hebrew at Cambridge under the legendary Henry Hart. Further study under Professor Winton Thomas and a year of research at the Hebrew University in Jerusalem confirmed me in my devotion to the 39 books of the Hebrew Scriptures, so much so that when, many years later, I was teaching at an Anglican theological college the word got around that I didn't know anything after the book of Malachi.

It is of course not entirely true because no classicist, let alone a Christian one, could fail to revel in the richness of New Testament Greek and want to read and expound it. But there is so much ignorance of, and sometimes antipathy to, the Old Testament that I have felt it to be my calling to do what little I can, through preaching and teaching, to make the Old Testament live for Christian congregations.

The first obstacle to overcome is getting people to believe that the Old Testament makes sense and is therefore worth taking the trouble to read. Problems of literary style, historical and cultural background, language and context also have to be addressed, and far too many would-be readers give up the unequal struggle for want of someone to guide them. As in the time of Pharaoh, king of Egypt, Hebrew midwives are needed to preserve the life of Moses and his successors for the present generation.

I have neither the time nor the skill to undertake this mammoth task. But a few sermons on Old Testament texts which carry a lasting message for Christian congregations may help a little. I hope so. Why, you may ask, on God's justice?

Partly because the Mowbray Preaching Series is launching into books of sermons on themes such as this and partly because the idea of God's justice is a favourite subject for Christian commentators but is not always grounded in biblical teaching. Hebrew justice is not the same as Roman justice nor is an appeal to God's justice the equivalent of demanding human rights, as is sometimes supposed.

I am very grateful to Douglas Cleverley Ford for his encouragement and advice, to say nothing of his skill in editing out some of my infelicities. Also to Mrs Lynn Bridger for the hours spent transferring my handwriting on to her home word-processor.

Biblical quotations are from the Revised Standard Version, unless acknowledgement is made. I still find it to be the best translation, combining accuracy with intelligibility.

John St Albans
Abbey Gate House
St Albans
1994

1
THE GOD OF JUSTICE

Far be it from thee to do such a thing, to slay the righteous with the wicked, so that the righteous fare as the wicked! Far be that from thee! Shall not the Judge of all the earth do right?

GENESIS 18.25

The other day I had a furious parent on my doorstep. Her son had been accused of a particularly unpleasant act and was on the point of being expelled from his school. He protested his innocence and she claimed she knew her son well enough to know that he would never do such a thing, but then all mothers say that. I got on to the headmaster and heard the story from him. A group of boys were working in the school library one Friday afternoon and when they had left, the lady librarian found on her desk a piece of paper obviously intended for her. It contained a crude, handwritten poem in the foulest of language, and she was going to resign unless the culprit was found and punished. The head had initiated an investigation and all the signs pointed to this particular boy. He had been one of the group, the handwriting was exactly like his and on a previous occasion he had been called to account for using obscene language. Although he denied responsibility, the headmaster was sure he was guilty and there was no alternative but to expel him. He could not let behaviour like this go unpunished. He had to make an example of the boy for the sake of the school. Mother was distraught. The boy stoutly pleaded innocence and demanded justice. The head was quite sure that justice was being done.

But where was justice to be found? Everyone had a different view. What was justice to the head was claimed by the boy to be gross injustice; and what the mother thought was unprintable. It was Easter and the boy was due to sit his A levels in June, and this could wreck his whole career. What was I expected to do to

1

secure justice for her, and was his story true? Or was the headmaster right?

The story had a happy ending. When the news of the expulsion got round the school, another boy confessed to the crime and clearly he was the guilty party. So he left, the boy and his mother received a fulsome apology, and justice was seen to be done.

Justice is one of the hardest things to achieve, as every parent, teacher and magistrate will agree. But everyone wants justice—for themselves and for other people. And there is nothing worse than being falsely accused of a crime you didn't commit—except being punished for it.

So I want to think about justice, not in one sermon but in many. For it has so many facets that it will take us a long time to come to terms with them all. And I want to begin with the Old Testament because that is where everything in the Bible begins; it contains the building blocks for Christian faith and morality.

I start with a story about Abraham. You may remember it. Three men (or were they angels?) called at Abraham's tent and were welcomed with typical Eastern hospitality. In return they forecast that Sarah, Abraham's wife, would have the son that they both longed for but no longer expected. But Sarah was well over age and she laughed at their words because the idea seemed so preposterous. We must not blame her for laughing: who wouldn't have laughed at such a thing? But in doing so she got the idea for the baby's name, for Isaac is Hebrew for laughter.

The three men were on their way to Sodom and they warned that because of the people's sins Sodom and Gomorrah were due for total devastation. God's justice demanded that the axe should fall. The end was nigh! Instinctively Abraham reacted. This could not be fair, because after all his nephew Lot lived in Sodom with all his family and they at least were not deserving that kind of punishment. Why should a just God destroy the righteous with the wicked? Why should innocent people suffer in the cause of 'justice'? He started to argue with God. It sounded more like haggling. He began by asking if God would really destroy everyone in the two cities if fifty righteous people could be found living in them. The Lord conceded the point and replied that for fifty righteous citizens he would spare the whole city. Abraham steadily cut down the figure in language reminiscent of an Eastern bazaar and got God down in stages from fifty to only ten righteous souls. It is here that we would have wanted him to try a last throw to see if the city would be spared for just five instead of ten, because that would have covered Lot's immediate family, but he does not—and we are left to wonder 'what if?'

It is a strange story told in very human terms and in language with which its first readers could readily identify. All the more important therefore that we must beware of being side-tracked by the incidentals. For instance, the God of Abraham is not a celestial market-trader whom we cajole and kow-tow to in turns. Prayer is not a question of persuading the Lord to do the opposite of what he intends doing. If this passage has anything to teach us about prayer, it is to do with what we may call 'exploratory prayer'. That means trying to find out God's will by a process of enquiry and exploration, which is something we still find ourselves doing when we are seeking God's guidance for our lives.

The one sure truth enshrined in this ancient story that we instinctively recognize is found in the wording of our text. 'Shall not the Judge of all the earth do right?' Far from being influenced by pressure or flattery, there is about the Lord, the God of Abraham, an essential justice. He is the Judge (in Hebrew *shophet*) and he can be relied upon to do justice (*mishpat*, the noun that describes what fair judges do). Here is an important Old Testament text and we need to look at it carefully. It contains four important truths.

GOD IS THE JUDGE OF THE WHOLE WORLD

This says as much about the nature of the world and the people in it as it does about its creator. It carries the implications of consistency and accountability. The universe is not at the mercy of haphazard forces: there is a divine controller who calls its inhabitants to account. Indeed the word *shophet*, judge, defines the action of one who rules, who issues decrees, who makes

3

decisions and to whom his creation will one day have to answer. He holds everything together. There is a pattern, an order in creation that emanates from him. He is supreme.

No human dictator therefore, however powerful, should be allowed to usurp God's authority, for he too will have to stand before the bar of God's judgement. A society that believes in God ensures that no individual can ever get away with having absolute and supreme authority. There is only room for one on the top rung of the ladder, and that is reserved for God. A godless society, on the other hand, is always prey to totalitarianism: the state, the party or the dictator takes the place of God and recognizes no authority higher than itself. That is why it is essential for human freedom that God's rule be recognized. Without it, liberation turns into tyranny.

GOD IS ESSENTIALLY FAIR

Written into the words of Abraham from which our text is taken is the concept of fairness. It is unthinkable, he says, that the Judge of all the world can be anything but just and do anything but what is right. A sense of fairness is an almost universal moral principle. The child at school can take punishment provided it is meted out fairly. The cheat who bucks the system, breaks the rules and gets away with it is rightly hated and despised. Even the criminal classes accept a fair cop and expect a fair trial, but woe betide the unjust judge or the 'bent copper'.

Abraham was appalled to think that God was being unfair. What justice was there in meting out destruction on two whole communities if the punishment of the majority inflicted suffering on the innocent few, whether that amounted to fifty or only ten? He could accept that a just God must punish wrongdoers, but he could not see why people like Lot should be caught up in their destruction. A fair point, and Abraham pressed it as far as he dared. In the event, of course, Lot and some of his family were rescued but they could save none but themselves in the process.

WE MUST TRUST GOD WHEN WE DON'T KNOW ALL THE FACTS

The judge in ancient Israel was not simply the man who decreed what was right and wrong. He was the one to whom people went with their complaints and arguments. After listening to both sides of the story, he it was who decided who was in the right and who was in the wrong. His job was to 'make the just man just and the guilty man guilty' (Deut 25.1). He therefore needed to be infinitely reliable. You had to be able to trust the judge. And if he made particularly wise decisions he was held in high esteem throughout the land.

The story of Solomon's wisdom in deciding between the two women who disputed custody of the child was a classic example of good judgement (1 Kings 3.16-28). It was a clever way of finding out who was the rightful mother and because of it Solomon's reputation knew no bounds. 'All Israel heard of the judgement which the king had rendered; and they stood in awe of the king, because they perceived that the wisdom of God was in him, to render justice.' If God could give this wisdom to his anointed king, how much more could he be trusted to be the righteous judge of all the earth. The knowledge that God was on the seat of judgement made people feel safe. There were not many human rulers of whom that could be said.

GOD'S JUSTICE IS TEMPERED WITH MERCY

If you go to the Central Criminal Court at the Old Bailey you will see the figure of Justice dominating the skyline overhead. She stands with a drawn sword in one hand, a pair of scales in the other and she is blindfolded. The message is clear. The scales weigh up the rights and wrongs, the sword punishes, and there is no favouritism. That is justice, Roman style. But Hebrew justice was different. Because the judge had to settle disputes, and many of these were appeals for help from the underprivileged against the tyranny of more powerful neighbours, the judge of Old Testament times was often seen as the champion of the innocent with a special concern for the poor—'the widow, the orphan and the stranger within your gates'. To them the judge was the defender of their rights, the protector against oppression, the one who could not be bribed.

So justice, Hebrew style, was 'He shall not judge by what his eyes see, or decide by what his ears hear; but with righteousness he shall judge the poor, and decide with equity for the meek of the earth' (Isa 11.3-4). Unmoved by signs of influence or sounds of power, the good judge gives the poor a fair hearing in every circumstance.

Shall not the Judge of all the earth do right? Yes indeed, and we look forward to the day when all nations will acknowledge his justice and mercy, when he comes to judge the living and the dead.

2

THE UPS AND DOWNS OF LIFE

The Lord was with Joseph, and he became a successful man.

GENESIS 39.2

When I have a few extra moments to spare I sometimes find myself opening my daily paper at the obituaries page. Not that I ever know any of the people they write about. Indeed I sometimes wonder how they qualify for the distinction when so much about them is so rarefied. Specialists in their field they may have been, but how did the newspapers ever hear about them, let alone find the right person to write up their lives?

But they are all successful, and most of them seem to have lived successful lives right from the outset. Scholarships here, prizes there, and achievements all along the line. If everything that is written is true, it hardly seems fair that people should live such charmed lives.

I expect the truth is that many of them had downs as well as ups, and that between the successes were a number of failures whose history has been kindly glossed over.

My subject today is undoubtedly a success story from the pages of the Old Testament. His epitaph comes in the last verse of the last chapter of the book Genesis which reads: 'So Joseph died, being a hundred and ten years old.' In ancient Egypt, where Joseph spent most of his days, they had no sophisticated system of keeping records but anyone who lived a complete and contented life was credited with a hundred and ten years. So the verdict on Joseph was that his was a successful life.

And this was despite the fact that he was hated by his brothers, sold into slavery, given up for dead by his father, accused of attempted rape, flung into prison and left there to languish with no one to plead his cause. If anyone was entitled to complain that life was grossly unfair for some, that person was

7

certainly Joseph. He has our sympathy. We all know something of what he felt.

HIS OWN FAULT?

Mind you, some of it was his own fault, nor was he helped by being picked out as his father's favourite. We remember him as the one of Jacob's twelve sons who was given a coat of many colours to wear, which suggests that he looked like a peacock among his hard-working, sheep-farming brothers. But newer translations describe it simply as a long robe with sleeves. That is much less colourful but it still suggests that Joseph was not specially equipped for hard manual work. No wonder his brothers were fed up with him.

Then there were the dreams. It would have been better if he had kept them to himself but why go up to your brothers and say, 'Hear this dream which I have dreamed: behold, we were binding sheaves in the field, and lo, my sheaf arose and stood upright and behold, your sheaves gathered around it, and bowed down to my sheaf'? Not much sensitivity, not much humility there. He should have realized he was asking for trouble. And then we read that at the age of seventeen he was shepherding the flock with his brothers and 'Joseph brought an ill report of them to his father'.

So here we have the successful Joseph introduced to us as a sneaky teenager, far too big for his boots and, to make matters worse, his father's pet. It was not long before the brothers got their revenge. Selling him to some traders who were on their way to Egypt was less messy than having his blood on their hands, though it was no difficulty to take back to Jacob a blood-stained cloak to give the impression that Joseph had met an accidental death from a marauding desert lion or leopard.

The young man had plenty of time to regret his thoughtlessness as he worked as a household slave in Pharaoh's Egypt. Missing his family and their tented, nomadic life he nevertheless adapted well to his strange surroundings and, as he had learnt to do with his father, he sought hard to please. Promotion, a position of trust, his master's high regard.

His good looks may have helped, as they often do; but they eventually proved his undoing, as they also often do. Potiphar's wife took a fancy to him and thought a slave would never dare to say no. He did, and we cannot but admire his integrity. 'How then can I do this great wickedness, and sin against God?' Would that more young people—and their parents too—would reject sexual temptation in as point-blank a way! It takes a great deal of courage to say no once. It demands real strength of character to go on saying no when the temptation persists. She pestered him day after day and finally compromised him when he was the only person in the house with her, and it was his word against hers.

INNOCENT VICTIM

Potiphar had to believe his wife's story, and when you read the story in Genesis 40 it doesn't seem as if Joseph even bothered to protest his innocence. He knew that, given his situation in his master's house, he hadn't a leg to stand on. No doubt he wondered if he should have taken the precaution of alerting Potiphar to his wife's improper advances at a much earlier stage, but who would have believed him in the face of her denials? And he had learnt his lesson about the likely consequences of sneaking to the boss. So he took his punishment on the chin and made the best of it in an Egyptian gaol.

By now our sympathies are firmly with Joseph. His less attractive characteristics have begun to be ironed out. He is now showing integrity and God is beginning to make a difference to his life. For the second time the Scripture says: 'the Lord was with Joseph', and Joseph was more obviously with the Lord too. So when two of his fellow-prisoners have dreams and look around for their meaning, Joseph restrains himself from setting up as an expert in dream interpretation and points them to God as the one who alone can understand what they are trying to say. You probably know the story. The chief butler has his job restored to him and the chief baker is executed, as Joseph predicted after listening to their dreams; and we all have high hopes that this will guarantee his speedy release from prison. 'Yet the chief butler did not remember Joseph, but forgot him.' And our hearts sink. He really does have the dice loaded against him.

LEARNING THE LESSONS

We must not spend too much time with the ups and downs of Joseph's life because our purpose is to learn what we can about the injustices of life. If you know what it is like to be accused of something you know you have not done, if your word has been disbelieved when you have been totally honest in what you have said, then you know a little of what Joseph went through. So what should you do?

(a) Admit that there have been times when the fault has been on your side. Maybe you did deserve a little of what you suffered. Maybe you should have thought more and spoken less, so as not to rouse others to jealousy or resentment. Maybe you are to blame for some of what went wrong. Few people are totally guiltless when a row is brewing and they are victims of hatred or persecution.

(b) No self-pity. When Terry Waite discovered that the tables had been turned on him and that from being a negotiator he had become another hostage, his first reflection as he faced the prospect of an endless captivity was to say to himself, 'No self-pity!' He knew it would be destructive of himself and his morale. He had to be positive. So, no recriminations, no self-pity.

(c) Integrity counts, even in prison. It is all too easy to behave like a criminal when you are branded one, or like a slave when you are sold as someone else's chattel. Joseph held his head high and tried to live in obedience to God under every circumstance. He was not going to be dragged down. He was still a servant of God even when he was the slave of man.

SUCCESS AT LAST

Eventually his chance came. His skill in interpreting dreams was remembered. He stood before Pharaoh and said, 'It is not in me; it is God who will answer Pharaoh . . . I cannot do it without him.' And he got it right: seven years of plenty to be followed by seven years of famine. A good administrator is needed; reserves need to be built up. A massive grain mountain must be created to see the country through the long years of stringency. Joseph is given the job and does it brilliantly. Success, success. From rags to riches, from prison to power in the land. And no one as much as looked at his c.v.

Now we have to be careful at this point. Nowhere in the Bible does God promise that we shall end up with a string of earthly honours. Or that innocent suffering will always turn into vindication and living happily ever after. That can only be guaranteed in the life to come. One day the injustices of life will be put right and balanced out, but you may have to wait until after death to experience it. Meanwhile the message of the Old Testament, as seen through the Joseph story, is 'In all your ways acknowledge him, and he will direct your paths' (Prov 3.6).

My reading of Joseph is that when he was down he accepted it as God's will. Not as God's punishment, perhaps as God's chastening, certainly as what God allowed for the time being. And in that faith he continued to live obediently to God, undeterred by his personal circumstances. I have a feeling that even if he had lived out his life in prison and never been released, he would still have kept his integrity, for the Lord was with him for better, for worse, for richer, for poorer, in sickness and in health, in prison or at liberty, in failure or in success. That would have been an obituary to be proud of, though I doubt if it would have been given many column inches in the *Egyptian Daily News*.

11

3
SAFE HAVENS

You shall select cities of refuge for you, that the manslayer who kills any person without intent may flee there. . . The man must remain in his city of refuge until the death of the high priest; but after the death of the high priest the manslayer may return to the land of his possession.

NUMBERS 35.11, 28

It was towards the end of the Gulf War that the phrase 'safe havens' began to gain currency. Saddam Hussein had been pushed back from Kuwait, his forces depleted and his military equipment reduced to a fraction of what once it had been. But instead of learning his lesson and returning Iraq to peace and stability, he turned against his own people and sought revenge on the minorities within his own national boundaries: the Shi'ites in the south and the Kurds in the far north.

We well remember the television pictures of long lines of Kurds fleeing into the mountains and making for the frontier into Turkey, terrified of Saddam's reprisals and a fresh outbreak of poison gas attacks. It was out of this that the British government (for I think we may take the credit for it) proposed the policy of providing a safe haven in northern Iraq for the Kurdish people.

Since then safe havens have caught the imagination of other politicians looking for a solution to other conflicts, in Bosnia and elsewhere. They are protected sites where beleaguered minorities can go and live out their lives in relative peace, surrounded by their own people and under international guarantees of safety. Undoubtedly, a good idea.

ACCIDENTAL DEATH

The Old Testament law proposed a similar pattern of safe havens for a certain class of Israelite citizen. They were called cities of refuge, and six of them were named, three on one side of the Jordan and three on the other. They were places where people could flee for sanctuary when they had accidentally been guilty of manslaughter and were escaping from retaliation. Numbers 35 deals with the circumstances surrounding the idea. First, the act of homicide must have been a genuine accident: an axe-head that flew off the haft and fatally wounded a bystander, or a javelin hurled while hunting which missed its target and killed another hunter. Secondly, the authorities in the city of refuge were to judge the genuineness or otherwise of the suppliant's plea for asylum. And thirdly, he must stay put within the bounds of the city; but not for ever, only until the death of the high priest. Then he can return home in safety.

Now this reflects a strange world of revenge and rough justice, far removed from the present day. Or so I thought until I met an old schoolfriend who was working for a large multinational company in West Africa. He told me that he had to travel hundreds of miles out in the bush but the company never allowed him to drive the company car. It always had to be a local driver. And the reason? Because if he was involved in an accident and a pedestrian was killed, the nearby villagers would immediately take their revenge on whoever was driving the car, *irrespective of who caused the accident*. Rough justice indeed. A life for a life, and why wait for the law to arrive because it never will?

It was a similar kind of rough justice that applied in the ancient Near East. Indeed it was thought to be the solemn duty of the next of kin of anyone who died an unnatural death, whether by murder, manslaughter or accident, to see that revenge was exacted in full. The blood of the dead man cried out for vengeance from the ground where it had been spilt. Read the story of Cain and Abel in Genesis 4, and remember the verse of that hymn which runs:

> Abel's blood for vengeance
> Pleaded from the skies,

> But the blood of Jesus
> For our pardon cries.

Long before the Lord Jesus shed his blood for us on the cross, there was this glimmer of grace in the provision of cities of refuge, the safe havens for the innocent victim of blood-guiltiness: God's way of escape.

Over the years devotional commentators on the Old Testament have interpreted the six cities of refuge in ancient Israel as a type of Christ. By this they mean that there was something strangely symbolic about those places of sanctuary, for they find their fulfilment, their 'antitype', in the person of Christ who is himself the way of salvation for all who flee to him for help. So the New Testament speaks of hiding in Christ, taking refuge in him, finding him to be a safe stronghold, or in Luther's words 'a mighty fortress', *ein feste Burg*.

A WAY OF ESCAPE

It seems to me that running like a thread through the whole of the Bible there is this theme of a way of escape. The Cain and Abel story ends with God putting a protective mark on Cain 'lest any who come upon him should kill him'.It was a mark of grace, given to a man who scarcely deserved it. The blood of the passover lamb smeared on the lintel and door-posts of the house, which saved the inhabitants of Egypt from the destroying angel, was another such mark of grace. And the same grace of God saw to it that there was a way out for those who did wrong in innocence in the cities of ancient Israel. All they had to do was to flee to the safe havens for sanctuary, and if they were genuinely innocent they would be genuinely safe from revenge.

Now is not this a thoroughly gospel theme? From time immemorial God has been providing his people with escape routes, ways of salvation. A God of grace would do no other. He does it for us in our temptations. St Paul writes: 'No temptation has overtaken you that is not common to man. God is faithful, and he will not let you be tempted beyond your strength, but with the temptation will also provide the way of escape, that you may be able to endure it' (1 Cor 10.13).

A man came to see me full of troubles. Everything seemed to have gone wrong. He could see no way out of his difficulties. 'I'm finished', he said. 'There's no point in going on.' 'No, you're not', I replied. 'There's a way out somewhere. There must be: there always is. Let's look for it together.' It was a response more out of hope than reality, but I could not believe that God would not help him to find his way through. If ever anyone needed a way of escape, that man did.

HOLDING ON

As it turned out there was no miraculous escape route. The way of salvation for him was simply to hold on to God, and God's promise to hold on to him. It was survival rather than flight. Endurance rather than escape. But even that can be our safe haven: God's provision of the capacity to survive. It is what the epistles mean when they speak of 'long-suffering'.

But of course the classic safe haven is Jesus Christ. Come to him, and you shall find rest for your souls. He is much more than a protector of the innocent. He offers pardon for the guilty too, if only they will confess their sins and ask for forgiveness. And those who hide in him and put their trust in him will be saved for eternity. What amazing grace that is! And it is God's provision for his fallen children, for people like you and me.

WIPING THE SLATE

You may think me fanciful but I cannot help noticing the phrase in our text about the need for the asylum-seeker to remain in the city of refuge until the death of the high priest. The impression is given that whenever the high priest dies it is the occasion for a general amnesty. A new chapter is opening and the old scores can be wiped off the slate. Then those in the cities of refuge can

15

go back home, and those who would otherwise be after their blood can let bygones be bygones and seek revenge no longer. Isn't there a parable here? For Christ was our great high priest, and though he allows us to come to him for salvation, it is because our high priest died that we can be doubly assured that we shall be safe eternally. 'Christ has died, Christ is risen, Christ will come again', we say. And we can go home in complete safety. For he is our safe haven, for time and for eternity.

4
AN END TO POVERTY

There will be no poor among you.

DEUTERONOMY 15.4

Our text today reads like a lorryload of wishful thinking. Undeniably, poverty is a bad thing. Everything should be done to eliminate it. It saps a person's vitality, drains his energy, drags down his self-esteem. Economists have set their minds to producing a poverty-free society, where everyone has sufficient and none are below the poverty line. Visions of Utopia have abounded, some more realistic than others. The Welfare State should have achieved a guaranteed minimum life-style for everyone in Great Britain and Northern Ireland, and yet we are told that there are millions still living in penury.

The natural reaction is to say: 'Well, it all depends what you mean by poverty.' Or else you compare the picture of poverty in the UK with the 'real' poverty of a Sudanese refugee and conclude that it is too relative a term to take seriously. But the fact remains that in our Western society, as well as in vast areas of the developing world, many, many people live in economic misery. They really are poor.

So how can the book of Deuteronomy blithely say: 'There will be no poor among you (for the Lord will bless you in the land which the Lord your God gives you for an inheritance to possess), if only you will obey the voice of the Lord your God'? Can this be anything more than wishful thinking? What lies behind such a confident declaration?

A JUST SOCIETY

The Law of Moses is more than a set of dos and don'ts. It had a vision. As a new life in a settled promised land was being prepared for, these early books of the Bible were sketching out how things could be. There were of course many regulations governing conduct and behaviour. But there was also a blueprint of a just society to which the children of Israel were to aspire. It may be dismissed as impracticable, but at least it was an attempt to express justice in economic terms.

And here we come to the principle of the sabbatical year and the year of jubilee. That is to say, every seventh year was an important milestone, and after seven times seven years there was to be a jubilee. But these were not simply an excuse for celebrations, they were times when slaves were released, property was returned to its original owner, debts were remitted and the fields lay fallow for a year.

'What', you may ask, 'has this to do with poverty?' Why, just this. The reasoning behind these measures was that land cannot be sold absolutely, for it belongs to God. And Israelites cannot be held in perpetual slavery, because they are the servants of God who brought them out of Egypt, the place of bondage. So, though a debtor who defaults may lose his freedom and his land, it cannot be forever, only for a limited period—until the next sabbatical year or, at the outside, the next year of jubilee. And in keeping with that idea, a man's land could really only be sold to someone else leasehold and never freehold. You sold your land not on the basis of its value as land but for the number of harvests that could be reaped before the next jubilee year was due.

Alongside this you have the prohibition on lending money at interest. This was explicitly forbidden between fellow-Israelites. 'If you lend money to any of my people who is poor, you shall not be to him as a creditor, and you shall not exact interest from him' (Exod 22.25). Indeed the taking of interest, or usury, was anathema to the Israelites. They could lend at interest to foreigners but not to their compatriots.

All this seems far removed from daily life today, and our pattern of fluctuating interest rates, bank loans and Barclaycards. However loyal we may want to be to the teachings of the Bible we find it impossibly difficult to conform to regulations such as these. Indeed, we cannot help wondering whether the Israelites themselves actually kept to all these commandments and prohibitions. How ever would it have worked out in practice?

SOCIAL EQUALITY

So let us come back to our text: 'There will be no poor among you.' What does seem clear is that the Old Testament tried very hard to work out a system of social and economic life which would prevent the growth of poverty and financial dependence. The ideal was a life of social equality. Whenever this was in danger of being distorted, there had to be checks and balances, and the chance of restoring the pattern to what it was before. The seven-yearly or jubilee adjustment provided this opportunity.

To my mind, it is futile to try to remodel modern Western economies on the basis of the laws of Moses, but that does not mean that we ignore what these Old Testament draughtsmen were trying to do. Their vision still has meaning for us today.

First, they believed fundamentally that God had called them to freedom. 'You shall remember that you were a slave in Egypt' but you have been set free, redeemed by God's gracious power. And now their new way of life was supposed to reflect that liberty. They were slaves no longer.

Secondly, they were of equal value in the sight of God. As children of Israel, they were God's special possession, and if God set such a high store upon them they needed to give respect to each other and not exploit one another.

And thirdly, major discrepancies of poverty and wealth, power and subservience, ownership and dependency, were not to be encouraged but actively resisted. They were not appropriate for God's redeemed people. So the fight against poverty had to be fought, and everything that enslaved had to be avoided. 'There will be no poor among you' was an ideal, an aspiration born out of religious conviction, that the Law of Moses held out to its Israelite readership.

Mind you, a few sentences later in Deuteronomy 15 we find the apparently contradictory words 'For the poor will never cease out of the land.' That is much more realistic! But it goes on: 'therefore I command you, You shall open wide your hand to your brother, to the needy and to the poor, in the land.' 'You shall give to him freely, and your heart shall not be grudging when you give to him; because for this the Lord your God will bless you in all your work and in all that you undertake.'

So here we are with a two-pronged assault on the demon of poverty. On the one hand, we are to demonstrate generous, practical charity—ungrudging, open-hearted. We owe such generosity to God and we pay it to his children. At the same time, we take to heart the example of the economic planners of ancient Israel and do all we can to ensure that poverty is not institutionalized. We strive to reform the system so that wrongs and evils can be righted, burdens can be relieved, and prison doors can be opened for the many who are enslaved to debt.

Those who are cushioned against today's financial pressures by a private income, a secure job or substantial savings in the bank, have no idea what it is like to be one of the thousands of 'no-hopers' who are daily dependent on meagre social security payments or who queue up at the doors of debt counselling bureaux, desperate to find a way out of their own kind of slavery. Rarely are they the victims of their own foolishness; more often than not their troubles are due to illness, redundancy, unforeseen circumstances which could strike anyone. They need more than sympathy. They need help. The chains need to be loosed. For though it is true to say with Moses that the poor will never cease out of the land, we are under obligation to Moses to pick up his vision of the day when 'there will be no poor among you'.

5
'AND A GOOD JUDGE TOO. . .'

You shall appoint judges and officers in all your towns which the Lord
your God gives you, according to your tribes; and they shall judge the
people with righteous judgement. You shall not pervert justice; you shall
not show partiality; and you shall not take a bribe, for a bribe blinds the
eyes of the wise and subverts the cause of the righteous. Justice, and only
justice, you shall follow, that you may live and inherit the land which
the Lord your God gives you.

DEUTERONOMY 16.18-20

St Albans has recently been supplied with a rather splendid, purpose-built Crown Court. On the day of the official opening by a distinguished Red Judge, representatives of all the legal fraternity crammed into the largest of the court-rooms for the formal ceremony. The bishop was invited to offer a prayer of dedication, and I felt very honoured to do so. It was an indication that the law recognizes that all justice stems from God and we are responsible ultimately to him. I was even more delighted when I later learnt that the carefully-worded prayer, over which my chaplain and I had wrestled long, had been photocopied and distributed to all the court officers for their future guidance.

In between times I talked with our resident judge and he reminded me of some of the cases he had tried in the old buildings, now used as magistrates' courts. I remembered one particularly painful occasion when he had been lampooned in the local press, quite unfairly, for one of his judgements. We had recently had the case of a four-year-old boy in Hemel Hempstead who had been abducted from a park and was missing for eight or nine weeks. The whole area had been searched, police frogmen had looked in every lake and gully and the little lad was almost given up for dead. Then he was found in his captor's room in a men's hostel, though no one knew how he had escaped notice and why he had not uttered a cry. The kidnapper was sent down for eleven years, reduced on appeal to seven.

Then came the case of a well-to-do housewife snatched from her home while she was ironing in the kitchen, gagged and trussed up like a chicken, and locked for 36 hours in the boot of a car before eventually being taken blindfolded to a room above a shop, also in Hemel Hempstead, and chained to a radiator. Her masked kidnapper meanwhile drove around the country telephoning menacing demands for an exorbitant ransom from her distraught husband. In the goodness of God the woman was discovered, her muffled cries being heard by an early milk roundsman and she was released. Her kidnapper was sent down for fourteen years.

Then the local press took over. What kind of justice was this, they asked? What sort of judge was it who valued the life of a little boy from a council house less highly than the wife of a wealthy businessman? This was the only comparison they drew, and the public outcry lasted for days—until they found something else to shout about.

TOTAL IMPARTIALITY

Now, I am quite sure that the sentences were just, given the full factors revealed in the two cases, but it came across to me as a classic example of public opinion's concern to see that there was never any suspicion of partiality in the operation of our legal system. People expect total impartiality of our judges. Everyone, high or low, is equal before the law. We would be horrified if it were any other way, and we like to pride ourselves that our judiciary is pretty well free of any bias or what the Bible calls 'respect of persons'.

The Old Testament had similar ideals. Indeed, that is the source of the standards we hold dear. 'You shall not pervert justice; you shall not show partiality; and you shall not take a bribe.' Make no mistake, it was not easy to maintain those standards three thousand years ago, and it is not particularly easy today either. Not when you are being bothered by public criticism after the event or apprehensive of it before you pass sentence.

Lord Edmund-Davies, famous for his trial of the Great Train robbers and for his presidency of the Aberfan enquiry, summed up the key quality needed of a judge in the one word 'valour'. He has to possess the courage to be independent, to face unpopularity, to follow the facts, to weigh up the evidence and to make up his mind without fear or favour. It must be a lonely job, and I felt for my resident judge as he showed me round the Crown Court and spoke to me of his work and its demands.

The text with which I began this sermon takes us back to the time of Moses, to whom most of Israel's institutions are traced back. It is no surprise therefore to read in 2 Chronicles about a revision of the nation's legal system under King Jehoshaphat. 'He appointed judges in the land in all the fortified cities of Judah, city by city, and said to the judges, "Consider what you do, for you judge not for man but for the Lord; he is with you in giving judgement. Now then, let the fear of the Lord be upon you; take heed what you do, for there is no perversion of justice with the Lord our God, or partiality, or taking bribes"' (2 Chron 19.5-7).

NO DELAY

We have said a great deal about the importance of *impartiality*, so we need not dwell on it any longer. But there are some other principles of the judicial system prized in ancient Israel which have meaning for us still. The first was *immediacy*. This lies behind the reference both in Moses and in the reign of Jehoshaphat to the appointment of judges in every town and city. There needed to be a man on the spot who could give the matter under dispute his immediate attention. Justice should not be kept waiting, or resentments fester, memories get reshaped and a relatively minor incident can too easily inflate itself into a *cause célèbre*. Justice long delayed is no longer justice.

I felt this most forcibly when I visited Bedford prison and

talked with some of the prisoners on remand and awaiting trial. One was suffering torments because he had been waiting nine months already on a charge of having murdered his twin brother. He protested to me that it was an accident, some high-spirited tomfoolery that went disastrously wrong, but for nine long months he had been suffering the agony not only of his twin's death but of the grief he had caused to his mother which he was incapable of doing anything to assuage. Even allowing for the need to prepare the case properly, I could not believe that he and his family were being treated justly. A long wait is the enemy of true justice.

The same is true of the application of the death penalty. Only yesterday I received a fax from Amnesty about a certain Gary Graham due to be killed in a few days' time by lethal injection, after having been on death row in his Texas prison for over ten years. Quite apart from his constant protests of his innocence, and the fact that he had been sentenced to death by only a 10–7 majority, what kind of justice is it that leaves it so long to exact society's revenge? Our every instinct tells us that here is something grievously wrong.

GOD'S JUSTICE

The second feature of Old Testament justice was its *religious dimension*. It did not have to be a priest in the judge's seat, though sometimes that applied; it could be a totally secular dispute that was being tried. But, said the scripture, 'you judge not for man but for the Lord'. This lifts the judge's task (and the jury's too) to an altogether higher plane. It suggests that the purpose of the court is not simply to sort out a wrangle in as fair a way as can be done, but that the court's task is to ensure that God's standards are being maintained in human behaviour. He is interested in the decisions because they should reflect his quality of justice. The court is engaged in divine service every time it sits!

Finally, please note that the administration of justice not only demands divine qualities but is supplied with divine grace. 'He is with you in giving judgement', says one of our texts. So 'let the fear of the Lord be upon you', is how it goes on. Yes, because as many a judge will admit, there are times when something more than merely human wisdom is needed. It is not a mark of weakness or incompetence for a judge to pray for help. If anything it is a sign of his stature, for he knows that he is doing a work for God and he combines his proper professional expertise and legal knowledge with an equally proper acknowledgement that he needs God's grace. As one of them put it: 'I pray because I'm not quite sure where my knowledge ends and where God's begins.'

But what does one pray for and how can you express it? Perhaps I can answer that by reading you the prayer I used for the opening of the St Albans Crown Court:

O God, the Judge of every human heart, we pray that this place may be a true house of justice where the ordering of human society is governed by the values of your eternal kingdom, where the upright are vindicated, the victim supported and where wrongdoing is exposed and condemned. We pray for all who (will) work here, that they will be inspired to serve a greater good; grant to all who minister justice the spirit of wisdom and discernment; and that they may be strong and patient, upright and compassionate, fill them, we pray, with the spirit of reverence and godly fear. And as your judgement is tempered with mercy, bless those who plead the cause of others and may those who are punished for their sins also find forgiveness and restoration through their Advocate in Heaven.
Amen.

6
AN EYE FOR AN EYE

Your eye shall not pity; it shall be life for life, eye for eye, tooth for tooth,
hand for hand, foot for foot.

DEUTERONOMY 19.21

Of all the texts in the Old Testament this must be one of the
most difficult. It is used to justify retaliation, almost irrespective
of the rights and wrongs of the matter: 'He hit me, so I hit him.'
It is quoted by those who want to draw a sharp distinction
between an Old Testament God of vengeance and a New
Testament God of love—which is of course a travesty of the
truth. It is wrenched out of its context to portray Judaism in a
bad light in contrast with Christianity and the teaching of Jesus
about turning the other cheek. So it is not the most promising of
texts for a sermon in church.

Now no one would deny that there is a contrast between parts
of the Old Testament and parts of the New. The Sermon on the
Mount refers to it. 'You have heard that it was said, "An eye for
an eye and a tooth for a tooth." But I say to you, Do not resist
one who is evil. But if any one strikes you on the right cheek,
turn to him the other also . . .' (Matt 5.38–39). But in the same
breath Jesus said that he had not come to destroy the law and the
prophets but to fulfil them. What did he mean?

PROPORTION

To answer this we must go back to the context in Deuteronomy,
which is all about crime and punishment. How does a God-
fearing society deal with violence and threats of violence? One
way is to say 'String 'em up and flog 'em'. And from time to time
the tabloids will be calling for that kind of punishment for a

particularly hideous crime. 'Teach the villains a lesson.' 'Hanging's too good for them.' 'Bring back the birch.' It is a very human reaction to an outrage that has been committed. It has its echo in the Bible, in the proud boasting of Lamech: 'Lamech said to his wives: "Adah and Zillah, hear my voice; you wives of Lamech, hearken to what I say: I have slain a man for wounding me, a young man for striking me. If Cain is avenged sevenfold, truly Lamech seventy-sevenfold"' (Gen 4.23–24). Nowhere in the Bible are Lamech's words commended. They are the language of the braggart, of the man who repays violence with even worse violence. This is not God's way. Instead we have an eye for an eye and a tooth for a tooth.

So here is the Old Testament advocating *proportionate response* as a cardinal feature of social justice. Disproportionate retribution is over the top and should not be allowed. Pickpockets should not be sent to the galleys; sheep stealers ought not to be hanged. Mercifully we have grown out of a system of penalties like that and have learnt instead the wisdom of the Mikado: 'Let the punishment fit the crime.'

The Old Testament also teaches the importance of a *limited response* to violence. It does not say that you *have* to inflict an eye for an eye and a tooth for a tooth. It is saying that that must be the maximum penalty. The desire for vengeance and retaliation has to be held in check. There is a point beyond which you may not go.

There is a third feature of Old Testament justice enshrined in our text. It is that retaliation is a *matter for the appointed judges*; it is not for private citizens to take the law into their own hands. Justice demands a measure of objectivity. Anger must not come into it, nor must pity. On this occasion the law wears a blindfold and acts impersonally. The law cannot forgive: it cannot be generous.

GENEROSITY

But people can. They do not have to extract the last penny or the last drop of blood. They can demand less than their due. This explains Our Lord's teaching in the Sermon on the Mount which we have just quoted. When he quotes the Old Testament law and then says 'But I say unto you', he is not negating the law, he is going back to its original meaning. He is switching the attention from the letter of the law to the spirit of the law.

So 'You have heard that it was said, "You shall not commit adultery." But I say to you that every one who looks at a woman lustfully has already committed adultery with her in his heart' (Matt 5.27–28). Jesus moves on from the adulterous action to the lustful look, from the sinful deed to the sinful disposition. And in the case of retribution for an injury, Jesus is similarly dealing with the vexed question of how you respond to personal injury.

The law said the response must be proportionate and limited: not more than an eye for an eye. The spirit of loving generosity says that the proportion could be less still, and if your enemy hits you on the right cheek you give him the other. If he sues you for your coat, you let him have your cloak as well. If he forces you to go with him one mile, you go with him two miles.

This is not pure justice. The courts could not operate in this way. But, Jesus insists, this is the direction in which the Old Testament law is leading you. This is the spirit of the law. I came not to annul the law but to fill it out.

Revenge can be a horrible thing. We see it working its way through a whole community in Northern Ireland. A bomb goes off in a crowded shopping precinct. A warning was given but it was never long enough. The police tried to evacuate the area but were not completely successful. A mother doing her weekly shopping was killed and her toddler was scarred for life. Anger and revulsion run through the whole community, not just the Protestants who recognize the hallmark of the IRA. Leaders appeal for calm and reconciliation. The next night three hooded gunmen knock at the door of an innocent Roman Catholic and gun him down before his terrified family. They claim it as justifiable homicide, a life for a life, evening up the score. But is it justifiable? No way. Indeed it is the sort of callous, cold-blooded action that arouses in every decent person the self-same feelings of fury and disgust that the bomb outrage provoked. Two wrongs don't make a right, we say. How, oh how, can we end this incessant cycle of murder and bitterness? Vengeance solves nothing. All it does is to perpetuate the hatred.

BREAKING THE CYCLE

Jesus knew this only too well. That is why he showed his followers an even better way. The way of absorbing the hatred by turning the other cheek, which was precisely what he did upon the cross. He soaked up men's derision and anger and desire for revenge, and silently let them abuse him to the point of death. It was the only way the cycle could be broken.

So don't use this text to justify your personal desire to get your own back on anyone. 'An eye for an eye' has nothing to say in your favour. Instead, look to the one who gave his back to the smiters and who let them wreak their hatred on him, so that he could defeat them by the power of sacrificial love.

Greater love has no man than this, that he lays down his life—*for those who hate him.*

7
WHAT TO DO WITH REFUGEES

You shall not abhor an Egyptian, because you were a sojourner in his land.

DEUTERONOMY 23.7

People of my generation remember the war years only too well. My own memories include their fair share of bombs and gunfire and wailing sirens, but I also remember the influx of people from overseas. Australians with their distinctive headgear, Poles with their broken English, and then the Americans with their inordinate wealth. At school too we welcomed boys and girls with German-sounding names, refugees from Nazi Germany, most of them separated from their parents and fostered out through the Save the Children Fund.

I say welcomed, but that is not strictly true. Schoolboys can be incredibly cruel and one of my most shameful memories is of a playground fight in which a group of boys held down a German Jewish boy while someone with a score to settle punched him in the face with the words 'Dirty Jew, filthy Hun'. I never knew what provoked the outrage but years later I discovered that the boy's parents and family had all been annihilated in the Nazi gas-chambers. I still wonder if he ever found it in him to forgive his persecutors—I mean, us.

What do you do with refugees? How should you treat them? In the nature of things they are different. They have a foreign accent or a coloured skin. They are not 'one of us' and can never be expected to be. It is hard to practise total lack of discrimination, try as you will. No amount of racial discrimination legislation, no amount of equal opportunities seems capable of doing away with injustice altogether. All we can do is try and try harder, and go on trying.

What does the Bible have to teach us? There is a refrain in the Old Testament which asks for special treatment for 'the

30

fatherless, the widow and the stranger within your gates'. The first two are understandable. They are your own kith and kin who have lost their bread-winner, the man of the house who can stand up for them and protect them from being put upon by an unscrupulous neighbour. We have more than our fair share of single-parent families to whom similar consideration needs to be given. The stranger within your gates is in a different category, however. He is the resident alien, the sojourner, who is part of the community, but has only limited rights. He is not yet a full citizen, and indeed may never be able to become one. He may not be a Jew. He may have come in as a migrant worker or perhaps he was a slave and won his freedom. But he was not a true-born Israelite. What do you do with him? He is a test case.

But it is not the alien who is on trial, it is the whole Israelite community. God is watching to see how they will treat him and they will be judged accordingly. So to help them pass the test, the Old Testament gives them some good advice.

PUT YOURSELF IN THEIR SHOES

'Remember that you were once a slave in the land of Egypt.' To most Israelites Egypt stood for the place that they had escaped from and never wanted to return to. It spoke of slavery, oppression, ignominy, and was the very antithesis of Canaan, the place of freedom and plenty and the right to own land, a land flowing with milk and honey. So Egypt and the Egyptians were avoided and hated.

But, said God, 'You shall not abhor an Egyptian, because you were a sojourner in his land'. You may not have liked it there; you were glad to get out of it. But you must never forget what you once were—a foreigner, a slave, a person without land, without rights. Go back there in your mind and remember those days. Then look at the people in your midst for whom Canaan is *their* Egypt, and be kind to them.

SAFEGUARD THEIR RIGHTS

The sojourner, the resident-alien (the Hebrew word is *ger*, rhyming with hair), was entitled to equality before the law. Moses said, 'I charged your judges at that time, "Hear the cases between your brethren, and judge righteously between a man and his brother or the alien that is with him. You shall not be partial in judgement; you shall hear the small and the great alike; you shall not be afraid of the face of man, for the judgement is God's"' (Deut 1.16–17). He also had many of the benefits of living in Israel. He could enjoy rest on the Sabbath day. 'In it you shall not do any work, you, or your son, or your daughter, or your manservant or your maidservant, or your ox, or your ass, or any of your cattle or the sojourner who is within your gates, that your manservant and your maidservant may rest as well as you' (Deut 5.14). The sojourner may have come well down on the list, even after the domestic animals, but at least he is mentioned. And a day free of work on the Sabbath was his inalienable right as well as his God-given duty.

The *ger* did not have the right to own land, however, and was dependent for his livelihood on hiring out his services, so he was usually poor and was classified with the widows and orphans and all who were 'economically weak'. All the more reason then that the Israelites should have been urged to make generous charitable provision for them with the gleanings after harvest and much besides.

I am not saying that the Old Testament got it completely right, but at least it pointed the way to where a God-fearing nation should be going. Any nation can look after its first-class citizens, but the acid test of a nation is the way it cares for those who for whatever reason find themselves marked down as second-class. It may be because they were not born here, or their parents weren't, or because they dress differently or are retaining their traditional culture, or simply because they lack an educated accent. Whoever they are, they are the people by whom a society is judged. Where, I wonder, do we come in this league? And if you are a first-class citizen yourself, I suggest you ask someone who isn't for their answer first.

LET JESUS BE YOUR EXAMPLE

St Matthew in his opening chapters makes much of the fact that the holy family fled from Bethlehem and Herod's soldiers, and sought refuge in Egypt. 'An angel of the Lord appeared to Joseph in a dream and said, "Rise, take the child and his mother, and flee to Egypt, and remain there till I tell you; for Herod is about to search for the child, to destroy him"' (Matt 2.13). No other gospel-writer noticed the point, but to Matthew it had meaning. Here was the infant Messiah sharing in the history of the people he had come to save, so that it could be said of him as was said of Israel: 'Out of Egypt have I called my son.'

Not only that, but throughout his years of public ministry Jesus renounced his citizen-rights and lived on the margins of the society he sought to serve. 'Foxes have holes and the birds of the air have their nests, but the Son of Man has nowhere to lay his head.' He was forever dependent on people with property to lend him—a boat, an ass, an upper room—because he had nothing of his own. In a way, he too was a sojourner in Israel.

A FINAL THOUGHT

When I went to Jamaica and other parts of the Caribbean to try to establish partnership links between their dioceses and St Albans, I was repeatedly told of the treatment given by the Anglican Church to that first generation of Caribbean immigrants who came to England in the 1960s and 1970s. It was an unhappy tale of rejection, misunderstanding and marginalization. However loyal the newcomers were as Anglicans they seemed invariably to have been sent down the road to the Pentecostal Churches, where it was thought (no doubt kindly) that they would feel more at home. It has helped to make the black-led Churches what they are today, but the Church of England has been gravely impoverished as a result.

So you may well have been thinking of those Caribbean brothers and sisters in Christ in terms of our subject today, for we have certainly consigned them to the margins of our cities and our society. But there is a wider meaning, and it is illustrated by that word 'Egyptian'. It is the word from which we derive the term 'gypsy', the travelling people who pitch their caravans, live their own way of life and are forever being moved on by the police and local authorities who would prefer them to be in someone else's territory.

But whether we apply these words of wisdom to them or to second-generation visitors from the Commonwealth, or to refugees from Nazi and other persecutors, or to present-day asylum-seekers, we have no option but to love them in the name of our Lord and to remember his words: 'Inasmuch as you did not do it unto one of the least of these my brethren, you did not do it unto me.'

8
A BIT OF A FIDDLE

You shall not have in your bag two kinds of weights, a large and a small. You shall not have in your house two kinds of measures, a large and a small. A full and just weight you shall have, a full and just measure you shall have; that your days may be prolonged in the land which the Lord your God gives you. For all who do such things, all who act dishonestly, are an abomination to the Lord your God.

DEUTERONOMY 25.13-16

It all began with a sermon I was preparing on the Book of Daniel and Belshazzar's Feast. You may remember the story of the writing on the wall (Daniel 5). King Belshazzar was feasting in his palace in Babylon with all his lords, drinking wine and praising the gods of gold and silver, and suddenly a man's hand appeared and wrote on the wall the words 'Mene, mene, tekel upharsin'. And it was Daniel who gave the interpretation: 'You are weighed in the balances and found wanting.'

I have never been very good at weights and measures. I can cope with how many pints there are in a gallon and how many pounds in a hundredweight, but the Bible always foxes me, with its ephahs and baths, its shekels and its minas. So I went to my favourite Bible dictionary to find out the meaning of these words. I soon discovered that there are fifty shekels (the Aramaic word is *tekel*) to a mina (Aramaic *mene*) and the *peres* (plural *parsin*) is the half-shekel. So what was written on Belshazzar's wall was the names of weights used to measure gold.

Now I tell you this not because I am going to preach about Daniel or Belshazzar but to tell you what I also discovered in the dictionary. For I read that ancient weights were stones carved in shapes, usually with a flat base which made them easy to handle, and that they were often inscribed with their weight and the standard which was being followed. But then I read (italics mine): 'Few Hebrew weights yet found of the same inscribed

35

denomination have proved to be *of exactly identical weight.*' I gasped. In an instant I realized why it was that the Old Testament kept on harping about honest weights and false balances. Especially when you remember that the street-trader was the man who carried his own set of weights in a pouch or wallet on his person and provided the scales as well.

Imagine the scene. You have gone to the market-place to buy some corn. Prices vary and so does the quality. You settle on the sack you want, haggle over the price and order three measures. You spread out your cloth on the ground and watch while the merchant fills his measure with the grain you have chosen. You watch carefully to make sure that it doesn't contain the sweepings of the threshing floor as well. The measure is filled to the brim and emptied out on to your piece of cloth. Once, twice, three times. You knot the corners together and then you weigh into the balances the silver pieces you are going to pay out. The scales are his and so are the weights. How can you trust him? Is he ripping you off? Has he got two sets of weights and is he using the heavy ones to get more of your silver than he should? You can never be sure. In the end you have to trust his honesty, but you watch him like a hawk. *Caveat emptor.* Let the buyer beware!

Into this kind of world the word of the Lord came with practical authority. 'A just balance and scales are the Lord's; all the weights in the bag are his work' (Prov 16.1). Or again, 'Shall I acquit the man with wicked scales and with a bag of deceitful weights?' (Micah 6.11). God's law was crystal clear. 'You shall do no wrong in judgement, in measures of length or weight or quantity. You shall have just balances, just weights, a just ephah, and a just hin: I am the Lord your God, who brought you out of the land of Egypt' (Lev 19.35–36).

Discovering all this, thanks to Belshazzar and a Bible dictionary, led me to thank God for our well-ordered society and for the Weights and Measures Act of 1963 and the network of local authority inspectors who make sure that standards are maintained in our shops and places of trade. And I think back to the days when I lived in the Middle East and was taught never to buy a tin of Nescafé without first turning it upside down to check that there was no tell-tale solder mark in the bottom

36

which would indicate that the contents had been removed and replaced with some cheap substitute!

But if we now live in a world where such abuses, if they should occur, are met with the full force of the law, what is the point—you may well ask—of preaching about them? The simple answer is that if God thought they deserved a mention in Old Testament times, it is highly likely that he still regards them as important today. These verses from Deuteronomy and elsewhere enshrine teaching about human behaviour and right conduct which has lasting significance. Let me tell you why.

BE SCRUPULOUSLY HONEST

Most people approve of honesty—generally. We expect people to tell us the truth and not to tell lies, though there are always white ones which we think excusable. We condemn in the strongest possible terms the massive City frauds we read about in the papers and we despise the Maxwells of this world for what they have done with their millions or, to be more accurate, with other people's millions. And we think that because we are not in the millionaire league we cannot be guilty ourselves. But the call is for scrupulous honesty. God knows that the big fraudster will get his come-uppance eventually. His concern here is with the person who massages the figures slightly, who rigs the scales so that no one notices, who tilts them in his own favour just sufficiently to gain a dishonest advantage.

I am sure you know what the word 'scrupulous' means. It is to do with scruples and a scruple is the smallest unit of weight, the equivalent of one 24th of an ounce. Its origin is the Latin word for a small pebble. So, you see, a call to scrupulous honesty is a call to be concerned with details. With pebbles rather than with boulders. And that touches us much more closely. How strict are we, for instance, in keeping our accounts or in charging our expenses? In filling up our income tax returns or in paying our bills on time? Believe it or not, God is interested in details like these.

ALWAYS GIVE VALUE FOR MONEY

There is a phrase in the Prayer Book version of Psalm 15 which always rings a bell with me and, I might say, brings the occasional twinge of conscience. It goes like this: 'Lord, who shall dwell in thy tabernacle: or who shall rest upon thy holy hill? Even he that leadeth an uncorrupt life: and doeth the thing which is right, and speaketh the truth from his heart.' And it goes on: 'He that sweareth unto his neighbour, and disappointeth him not: though it were to his own hindrance.'

Every promise that passes through your lips, every business deal you strike, every transaction you make, is a covenant sealed by the word of your mouth. Keep it sacred. Give full value.

The same thing applies to the covenants you make with God. The prophet Malachi had some strong things to say about 'the cheat who has a male in his flock and vows it, and yet sacrifices to the Lord what is blemished'. We know exactly what he meant. When we were at our wits' end we pleaded with God for help and made all kinds of promises if only he would come to our aid; and then everything turned out all right and we salved our consciences by putting an extra pound in the collection and forgetting what we said we would do. And we kid ourselves that God won't notice . . . What kind of honesty is that?

NEVER ABUSE A POSITION OF TRUST AND POWER

The man with the weights and the scales is the man with power. He can use them honourably or dishonourably, to his personal advantage or as an honest steward of the responsibility he carries. The same applies to the council officer or civil servant who has the power to award a major contract out of public funds. Too often such people have fallen prey to inducements and favours from over-eager tenderers. The more power you have, or are thought to have, the more temptations come your way. Often they are hidden beneath the respectable word 'commission'. Its ugly name is bribery.

St John's Gospel drops a large hint that Judas's downfall may have been to do with his being the keeper of the disciples' purse. He complained at the waste of Mary's expensive jar of ointment, poured over Jesus' feet, and calculated how much better it would have been for the three hundred denarii to have been given to the poor. But to quote John 12: 'This he said, not that he cared for the poor but because he was a thief, and as he had the money box he used to take what was put into it.' No doubt he was more subtle about it than those words imply or he would soon have lost the job, but it only needed a little carelessness here and a little muddle there and no one need be any the wiser.

So, if you have access to other people's money, however small, be warned! Never count the collection alone. Have all those accounts audited. Be open and above-board—and business-like—in everything. You cannot be too careful.

Which brings us back to Belshazzar's feast and those words, 'Mene, mene, tekel upharsin'. Yes, they were weights, and like our pound stood for both a weight and a sum of money. It was Daniel's genius to link the words with their meanings. *Mene* can also mean 'to measure', and *tekel* 'to weigh'. You are weighed in the balances and found waiting.

The merchant does not set out his weights in the scales only for the sake of his customer. He is also, without realizing it, weighing out himself and his integrity under the all-seeing eye of the God of justice.

9
APPEARANCES ARE DECEPTIVE

And Samuel said to Jesse, 'The Lord has not chosen these.'
1 SAMUEL 16.10

When I became a bishop I was told that the most important job I had to do was to make good appointments. 'It's not what you achieve yourself', my informant went on, 'but the people you leave behind you that really count.' I am not sure that I agree with him but the fact that I am recording that conversation many years later indicates at the very least that I remembered what he said.

The plain truth is that making good appointments is not at all easy. How can you be sure that you have chosen the right person? Are those glowing references to be trusted? How will he or she grow into a job they have not done before, in a context that is new to them? Are there any flaws in their character that do not appear now but may emerge later on? How does one assess potential?

CHOOSING A KING

Our text today comes from a passage in the Old Testament where the prophet Samuel was given the task of choosing out and anointing a new king for Israel. But it was not quite as simple as that. For one thing, there was a king in the post already, named Saul, whom Samuel had anointed, we are told, just six chapters previously. And furthermore the prophet's task was not to conduct an election nor yet to interview and select a candidate, but to tune in to what God wanted and try to discern his will for the people. In a word, Samuel had to spot the one whom God had already chosen. That at least is how the episode is described in 1 Samuel 16. But there are a number of ways in which God's will can be discerned. At the crudest level, you can discover it by the equivalent of spinning a coin—provided you pray first! Casting lots was the way in which King Saul had been picked out. Centuries later the early disciples used a similar method to choose a replacement for Judas in the company of the twelve after he had betrayed the Lord. Maybe if they had waited until after the Day of Pentecost they would have given the matter more careful reflection, guided by the Spirit, and chosen the apostle Paul instead, but that's another story. The fact is that in Acts 1.26 the lot fell upon Matthias.

But discerning God's will is much more than rolling the dice and trusting God to see to it that they end the right way up. Our God-given judgement needs to be brought into play as well, and this is what Samuel sought to do when he went down to Bethlehem to meet Jesse and to look at his sons. We have no idea why it was to Bethlehem that he went or why Jesse's family was his first port of call. All we are told is that the Lord had revealed this much to the prophet, but apparently nothing more. So the interviews began, starting with the eldest son Eliab.

You probably know the story. As Eliab stood there, Samuel thought, 'Surely the Lord's anointed stands before me'. But the Lord said to Samuel, 'Do not look on his appearance or on the height of his stature, because I have rejected him; for the Lord sees not as man sees; man looks on the outward appearance, but the Lord looks on the heart'. So along came number two, Abinadab, then Shammah, and eventually all seven sons were presented to Samuel and found wanting. And Samuel had to swallow hard and say to Jesse 'The Lord has not chosen these'. And he might well have gone back home to Ramah to await further instructions if he had not thought to ask Jesse if he had any other sons he could meet. And of course out from the fields came the boy David, and he proved to be just the person Samuel was looking for.

HOW DO YOU KNOW?

But how did Samuel know? The Bible story tells us that David was the youngest son and that he was ruddy, meaning fresh-complexioned or maybe red-haired. He had beautiful eyes and a handsome appearance—which rather suggests that Samuel *was* going by his looks and not by his character. What was more important was the prophet's intuitive sixth sense. It told him that this was the object of his journey, the person whom he had been sent by God to find and to anoint.

I am not convinced we can apply too much of this story to present-day selection procedures in the Church. After all, why restrict candidates to one village and one man's family in that village? But some principles surely apply, and the chief one is summed up in that saying, 'The Lord sees not as man sees . . . the Lord looks on the heart'. It goes without saying that outward appearances can be deceptive. Eliab's seniority as the eldest son was not decisive, nor was his commanding stature nor was his impressive appearance. The current king, Saul, had been chosen partly because he was head and shoulders taller than his peers but this had not guaranteed him success as ruler over Israel. Indeed it may have encouraged the arrogance which led him to behave independently of Samuel and so disobediently to God.

David, on the other hand, though good-looking, was a mere juvenile with a lifetime of development ahead of him. He had learnt submission through being the youngest of his father's sons and yet had shown himself capable of taking responsiblity for the family's flocks. So even at the human level he had much going for him, which a wise man like Samuel would have weighed up. But the decisive vote came from the inner voice of God in Samuel's heart, 'This is the man'. He had no need of references, still less of Myers-Briggs testing. He had discovered God's will.

Now the same principle that applies to making right appointments can be extended into other spheres. For we in our judgements, of situations as well as of people, need to be on our guard against judging by appearances. Things aren't what they seem to be. We have to apply our mental stethoscopes to the heart of the matter, so that we can feel the pulse and sense the inner realities hidden away behind the outward appearances.

CAREFUL SCRUTINY

Nowhere is this more necessary than in matters to do with social justice. There are so many apparently worthy causes pleading for our support, so many urgent needs competing for our attention, so many social issues calling for us to be engaged with them on behalf of securing justice for the afflicted or under-privileged. Most of them are no doubt genuine and respectable; some will probably be of doubtful validity. Careful scrutiny is required lest we find ourselves wasting our slender resources of time and money or, worse still, getting caught up in a charitable confidence-trick of the kind that has recently been in the news. The Lord looks on the heart; and his servants need to do the same.

Let me end with an illustration. A young ordinand was wanting to extend his limited experience and hoped to spend a year in a developing country, perhaps doing voluntary work in an Anglican diocese. I spoke about him to a friendly bishop. I gave him his c.v. with its good education, his degree in theology, his desire to serve, his Christian commitment, etcetera. The bishop was unimpressed. 'What is he like with people?' I told him that he was a gentle, kindly person who once surprised his friends by entertaining three elderly widows in the congregation to a meal that he had cooked for them in his own flat. 'I'll see him', said the bishop. And sure enough he took to him and invited him to spend a year in his diocese. 'Anyone can do a degree in theology', said the bishop, 'but only a man with a pastoral heart will invite three elderly ladies to dinner.'

For a discerning bishop that was the sign of a range of human qualities that no c.v. could point to. He spotted a character that cared for people and he knew that a young man like that was genuine and would never let him down.

There then is the spirit of discernment that I would dearly like to learn, so that I make good appointments, take up good causes, support the right organizations, and tackle the issues that really do need to be addressed. It is not the outward appearance I need to look at, but the heart of the matter that God wants me to see into.

10
FOUND OUT

Nathan said to David, 'You are the man.'
2 SAMUEL 12.7

Memories of guilt last a very long time. My mind goes back to a family holiday in Southwold many years ago. It was the year when England won the World Cup; it was that long ago. One sunny morning I was allowed to go off by myself to play a round of golf. 'You won't wear your studs in the house, will you?' warned the landlady. 'Wouldn't dream of it', I replied, as I drove off in my outdoor shoes.

Eighteen holes and a gasping thirst later, I threw my golf-bag and shoes into the boot and drove straight home with my spiked golf-shoes still on my feet. I clumped up the crazy-paving garden path to the open front-door and the stone staircase up to our rooms. 'Quite safe', I said to myself, and with one step over the threshold and on up the stairs I was in my room in no time and changing for a welcome bath. It had been a good morning.

Later that day the landlady confronted me. 'You wore your spikes', she said accusingly. 'Look!' And there between the front door and the bottom stair I saw to my horror the neat imprint of five holes matching the pattern of the sole of my left golf-shoe. The flooring was soft cork.

Shame and confusion! I didn't know where to put myself. I had been found out. And the holes are probably still there if you enquire at number — North Street (I wouldn't want the lady troubled with a constant stream of visitors).

Now, I would never have remembered that incident if I had not been found out. It would have been a totally unmemorable foot-fault! But I still feel bad about it. That is what a guilty conscience does for you.

A TRAGIC STORY

Today's text is about a much more grievous sin, combining adultery with murder, plus a whole catalogue of the deceit and shamelessness that all too often accompany them. It is the tragic story of David and Bathsheba.

David was a married man, though not happily. The love that had bound him to Saul's daughter Michal had gone sour, and nothing is known of Abigail and Ahinoam, both of whom had become his wives at some stage in his past. Instead he sought refuge in outdoor pursuits, notably leading Israel on the battlefield against old foes round about. The camaraderie of war was some compensation for the lack of companionship at home.

Our story begins with a break in the routine. 'In the spring of the year, the time when kings go forth to battle, David sent Joab, and his servants with him, and all Israel; and they ravaged the Ammonites and besieged Rabbah. But David remained in Jerusalem' (2 Sam 11). Rabbah, incidentally, or Rabbath Ammon to give it its full title, is the modern city of Amman, capital of the Hashemite Kingdom of Jordan. So conflict in the Middle East is not a modern invention. David stayed at home, and while he was walking on the roof of his house in the afternoon sun he saw a woman bathing, and she was very beautiful. He enquired about her and was told 'Is not this Bathsheba, the wife of Uriah the Hittite?' and without more ado he sent messengers and took her.

It is really no excuse to say that kings could do that in those days, any more than that pop-stars or television producers or cabinet ministers can do that in these days. The fact that it may have gone on, and that there were few constraints to prevent it happening, does not make adultery morally acceptable, now or then. The kings of the past, like the kings of the present, may have got away with it because there was no one to censure them, but God's judgement on such behaviour was defined long years ago in five words: 'Thou shalt not commit adultery.' There are no exceptions. None.

What followed only compounded David's dishonour. Not only did Bathsheba conceive, but we discover that Uriah was out on the battlefield with Joab and the army, a faithful soldier of an unfaithful king. David issued instructions that he was to be allowed home to report back to him and to have some home leave. No doubt he thought the child could then be attributed to Uriah and not to him. But the more he tried to persuade him the more determined Uriah was. 'My lord Joab and the servants of my lord are camping in the open field; shall I then go to my house, to eat and to drink, and to lie with my wife? As you live and as your soul lives, I will not do this thing.'

Uriah's dedication proved to be his death-warrant. David gave orders to Joab to put him in the forefront of the battle and then to leave him on his own to be killed by the enemy, and so it turned out. As far as David was concerned, the problem had been solved. Bathsheba could mourn and then he could bring her to his palace and make her his wife; and his son would be legitimate. What could be more satisfactory? All extra-marital affairs are a bit messy, but this one had been handled with real skill, and things had turned out well for everyone—except Uriah. But the story ends with the laconic statement: 'The thing that David had done displeased the Lord.' As if we didn't know.

A GUILTY CONSCIENCE

One of the shocking things about the story is that David still did not appear to have a guilty conscience. All his energy was being put into handling the affair and he did not allow himself to face up to matters of right and wrong. To him it was a matter of arranging and getting. He was a skilled manipulator and he probably prided himself on his success. He finished up precisely where he wanted to be. The sign of a good manager.

Then along came Nathan for an interview. 'I have a problem, and would like your advice', he said. 'Sure', said David, 'tell me all about it. I'd be happy to help.' His confidence in his managerial skills knew no bounds. Nathan went on: 'There were two men in a certain city, the one rich and the other poor. The rich man had very many flocks and herds; but the poor man had nothing but one little ewe lamb, which he had bought. And he brought it up, and it grew up with him and with his children; it used to eat of his morsel, and drink from his cup, and lie in his bosom, and it was like a daughter to him. Now there came a traveller to the rich man, and he was unwilling to take one of his own flock or herd but he took the poor man's lamb and prepared it for the man who had come to him.'

It was a story to enrage anyone with a sense of justice, and David rose to the bait. Note that despite his lack of a conscience over what he had done to Uriah and Bathsheba, he still retained a moral sense. Indignation welled up in him to affirm his self-righteousness. He knew where the high moral ground was and he was determined to stand firmly upon it. 'As the Lord lives, the man who has done this deserves to die. There's nothing I detest more than injustice, bullying, oppression, hypocrisy . . .'

Then Nathan said quietly to David, 'You are the man'. He did not need to say much more, but he said it. 'Thus says the Lord, I anointed you king over Israel and I delivered you out of the hand of Saul . . . Why have you despised the word of the Lord, to do what is evil in his sight?' And he went on to charge him with what he had done to Uriah and his wife, and pronounced God's judgement upon him.

David could have flown into a rage and sent Nathan packing. It is at least to his credit that he responded with the words 'I have sinned against the Lord'. We would have liked to hear a much fuller expression of penitence and self-loathing, but maybe that was concealed behind the bare bones of the story. Suffice it to say that David accepted the rebuke and his dormant conscience was roused to admit his guilt. No doubt he felt guilty too, and the anger he had directed out at the rich man in the parable was now directed at himself.

FASTING AND PRAYER

What a ghastly thing to have done! The enormity of it gradually forced itself upon him. What sort of a king was it that would use his power in such a despicable way! What kind of example was he to his people? And how could such animal behaviour be squared with all his practical expressions of piety and devotion to God? The quickened conscience finds tender spots everywhere and spares you nothing. David spent a week in fasting and prayer. It is said that the great penitential Psalm 51 was written as a result of his experiences of guilt and shame.

> I know my transgressions, and my sin is ever before me.
> Against thee, thee only, have I sinned, and done that which is evil in thy sight . . .
> Create in me a clean heart, O God, and put a new and right spirit within me.
> Cast me not away from thy presence, and take not thy holy spirit from me.

I wonder what would have happened to David if the Lord had not sent Nathan to him. Or if he had attempted to stifle his conscience and brazen it out, standing on such kingly dignity as he had left. He would never have made it to be a man of God, a worthy founder of a dynasty of kings and ancestor of the Messiah.

So, thank God for a sensitive conscience and for Nathan's bravery and skill in rousing it to life. Guilt feelings are some of the most painful that we have to endure, but we need them. They bring us low (where we often need to be) and they enable us to grow, through the experience of God's grace and forgiveness, to a greater holiness, as we pray with David 'Wash me and I shall be whiter than snow'.

11

THE WISDOM OF SOLOMON

And all Israel heard of the judgement which the king had rendered; and
they stood in awe of the king, because they perceived that the wisdom of
God was in him, to render justice.

1 KINGS 3.28

Today we are going to look at a great king who became a byword
for wisdom. Solomon. But his was not the wisdom of an
academic but the wisdom of a judge. For leadership in all its
forms is not so much about how much you know, though the
more you know the better, but about how you make decisions
and handle difficult situations. Call it tact or diplomacy, call it
common sense or *savoir-faire*; in Hebrew it was wisdom. And
the wise were people who knew what to do and could give good
advice to others or could act on it themselves.

CHOICES

The episode begins with a dream. 'At Gibeon the Lord appeared
to Solomon in a dream by night; and God said, "Ask what I shall
give you."' That is worth pausing over. For we usually think of
prayer as asking for things from God—and often not getting
them and then complaining, or wondering what has gone
wrong. Here God takes the initiative: 'Tell me what you would
like.' The context of the dream looks as if it was either
Solomon's wedding or his coronation, but in either case it would
have been a time for presents, and for thinking about them. So
what would Solomon like to have from God?

All sorts of thoughts passed through his mind, as they would
yours and mine. How marvellous to have a free dip at the divine
bran-tub! The very first thought was to ask for *a good long life,*

49

which was something highly prized in a society where longevity was the exception rather than the norm. In those days no one planned for retirement. You could do no more than pray you would be spared an untimely death from plague, famine or violence, three enemies that always stalked the land. And with no bright hope of life after death, but at best a shadowy continuance, life was a very precious commodity, and the longer it was the better. So that would certainly have been a reasonable request to make of God.

MONEY IS NEUTRAL

The next possibility was to ask for *wealth and possessions*. These were as much in demand then as they are now. The acquisitive instinct is powerful in all of us and there is hardly a person on earth who has not daydreamed about what they would do if they won the pools or married money or inherited a fortune. Now, let me make it quite clear that money is not of itself evil. It is not the root of all evil, as some people say. The Bible quotation they are referring to says that it is the *love* of money which is the root of all evil, not the money itself.

Money is neutral: it can be a good thing or a bad thing. The problem is not with the money but in the hearts of men and women who have it or desire it. That is where the corruption lies. People set their hearts on it, scheme to obtain more of it, accumulate it, seek security in it, grasp it in their fists, steal it and cannot bear to be parted from it. That is where the corruption lies. That is evil: what the Bible calls 'covetousness'.

Against this Jesus taught his followers, 'Take no thought for your life, what you shall eat and what you shall drink, and what you shall wear. The life is more than food and the body than clothing. But seek first the kingdom of God and his righteousness, and these things shall be added unto you.' And to the rich young ruler who not only had wealth but loved it too much, he said 'Sell what you have and give to the poor and you will have treasure in heaven'.

Solomon of course did not have the benefit of Christ's

teaching a thousand years later, but he resisted the temptation to be wealth-orientated, even though in the event he was blessed with very great wealth. But at the outset of his reign it was not his first priority.

A HEADY POTION

The third possibility was *power*. Power over other people's lives. A king would have a considerable degree of power, but there is all the difference between using the power you have responsibly and being power-hungry. The lust for power strikes all kinds of people, high and low. Sometimes those who have least of it long for it most. It can be a heady potion. In my view no one should be entrusted with it unless they have first shown that they can handle a modest amount without it turning their heads.

Mind you, there are many who have power and influence without ever being conscious of it. You do not have to stalk the mythical corridors of power (I have never discovered quite where they are) to be a person of influence. The parent or grandparent, the teacher, the youth leader, the journalist, all are people with power—for good or for ill. But Jesus' words about power have turned our understanding of it upside down. 'He who would be first among you', he said, 'must be the servant of all.' The only power that is incorruptible is the power of lowly service. Today's best example is Mother Teresa.

Finally, after dismissing all these possibilities, Solomon settled for wisdom. Listen to the modesty of his address to God: 'I am but a little child; I do not know how to go out or come in. And thy servant is in the midst of thy people whom thou hast chosen, a great people, that cannot be numbered or counted for multitude. Give thy servant therefore an understanding mind to govern thy people, that I may discern between good and evil.'

Not surprisingly the Lord was pleased with his choice. 'Because you have asked this, and have not asked for yourself long life or riches or the life of your enemies, but have asked for yourself understanding to discern what is right, behold, I now do according to your word.'

Thus ended the dream. Then reality burst in in the form of two quarrelling prostitutes. Solomon's heart must have sunk into his boots. Could they not have left him with his spiritual vision, his ecstasy, just a little longer? It rarely happens like that in real life. He had to sit in judgement in a tiresome dispute brought by tiresome people.

I hardly need to recount the story. Two women sharing a house; two new-born babies; one dies and they both claim that the living one is their own. No witnesses to give evidence. No identity tags. Her word against hers. How does that kind of problem get resolved? Which is the real mother and which one is lying? Solomon called for a sword and gave instructions for the living child to be divided in two, so that each could have half. For a brief moment the false mother accepted the logic of the decision. If she had lost her baby why shouldn't the other mother lose hers as well? That would even the score. The other screamed out in desperation to save her child from death. Better let the impostor have it than that the child should die. Solomon had his answer. The genuine mother had shown her love and was given back her baby. 'And all Israel . . . stood in awe of the king, because they perceived that the wisdom of God was in him, to render justice.'

It is quite a remarkable story and must have been a favourite for story-tellers from the earliest times. At one level it was evidence that God had answered Solomon's prayer. But at a deeper level it was an indication that justice was not a matter of merely making good decisions. First the truth needed to be uncovered, and a high degree of skill or wisdom was needed to get at the truth. A judgement had to be based upon a full knowledge of the facts, and that was not always easy to come by.

The same is true of social justice. I was recently invited, nay pressed, to espouse the cause of someone who was clearly the victim of high-handed action by representatives of the Home Office. The case, as put to me, seemed clear-cut. No one with a Christian conscience could honourably hang back from giving it his support. The least one could do was sign a petition, maybe write a letter to an MP or the Home Secretary. I had a sneaking doubt, possibly because the case was so crystal clear. Truth is rarely so transparent. I made enquiries. Gradually a very different picture began to emerge. Things had been done which did not appear in the submission. The victim was not as innocent as the papers suggested him to be. The campaigners were either naïve or had an ulterior motive. I put the correspondence in the waste-paper bin without a twinge of conscience.

Cases do not always end up like that. Bureaucracy can be a heartless tyrant, and we have not forgotten that just occasionally a Home Secretary has been found guilty of contempt of court if not actually of injustice. The point I am making is that justice must be preceded by wisdom, and wisdom is all to do with finding out the facts and weighing them up. That kind of wisdom is a gift from God.

Therefore to those who campaign, and rightly so, for social justice, I say 'Be wise'. Not every plausible story is true. You are almost certain to be criticized for being biased but try not to be criticized for being naïve. Instead, ask for a touch of Solomon's understanding mind, that you may discern between good and evil. Then there is a good chance that you will win the day.

12
COMPULSORY PURCHASE

But Naboth said to Ahab, 'The Lord forbid that I should give you the
inheritance of my fathers.'

1 KINGS 21.3

Until recently my daughter lived on a brand-new estate in
Staffordshire. Well-built detached houses. Double garages. Four
bedrooms. The property developer's delight, though because of
the recession they finished up by selling them almost on bended
knee to anyone who showed a spark of interest. The developer
managed to retain many of the features of the original farmland:
ancient hedges, a small stream, a pond where once the cattle
came to drink. It was a clever interweaving of old and new.

And in the middle of these smart executive houses was a
dilapidated farmhouse beside an even more down-at-heel barn
and outbuildings. I knew at once what its story was. The farmer
had to sell his fields but was determined not to give up his home.
So he endured the discomfort of being surrounded by a building
site, with all its noise and mud and lorries, for year after year
until the development was completed. He was a brave and
probably a very stubborn man. But he had the choice.

NO CHOICE

Today's story of Naboth and his vineyard was about a man who
had no choice. He had his rights but they were not sacrosanct in
the face of kingly power. So let me introduce the three main
characters in the plot.

First there was Ahab, king of Israel or Samaria. He was a
powerful monarch, a good strategist and a grandiose builder.
His ivory-decked palace in Samaria was a byword for splendour.

He loved power and enjoyed his unfettered freedom. Then there was his wife, Jezebel, a bad influence if ever there was one. It was a political alliance; her father was king of Sidon and priest of the sex-symbol goddess Astarte. So she had little sympathy for the austere worship of the Israelites. She too became a byword but not for splendour, more for barefaced cunning and brutality. Finally there was Naboth, Israelite yeoman stock to his fingertips; conservative, god-fearing, traditional.

The plot in 1 Kings 21 is about the abuse of power. Ahab, true to type, wanted to extend his palace grounds and the only thing that stood in his way was Naboth's neighbouring vineyard. He proposed an exchange or a purchase—all very reasonably. Naboth said no, flatly. The land had been in his family for generations. It was the family's inheritance, a sacred trust that he had received from his father and was duty-bound to pass on to his successors. The matter was not negotiable, king or no king. No sale.

If the story were not so tragic, the next part would be almost laughable. The great king 'lay down on his bed, and turned away his face, and would eat no food'. He sulked. Like many a powerful man who enjoyed his bombast, he was a child at heart. If he couldn't get his way he sulked. He probably stamped and slammed doors as well.

A good wife would have told him to snap out of it, or would have given him a different perspective. But not so Jezebel. She was already scheming ways of pleasing her husband and getting him what he wanted. She cared nothing for the people's traditions. After all, they were not her people and their God was certainly not hers.

HUMAN RIGHTS

Now this was much more than a dispute about property or about a compulsory purchase order. It was to do with human rights, and in Naboth's case these were inalienable. Even if he had wanted to sell there was something in Israel's religious constitution that told him it would not be right. By selling he would be dishonouring his family, past and future. He could not do it, and no one had the right to make him.

Claiming human rights can sometimes be a cover for maintaining personal prejudices, the not-in-my-backyard mentality. We need to be sure of our ground and not debase the concept. But if right is on our side, as it was for Naboth, God is with us in our stand for the dignity and honour of defending those rights and freedoms.

This does not necessarily mean that we shall win. Power that is thwarted can be incredibly brutal. And Jezebel responded to Naboth's bravery with a murderous plan. She knew that the property of rebels and public criminals reverted to the crown. So what could be simpler than to use royal power to dispose of Naboth on a trumped up charge of blasphemy and high treason. From the times of Exodus, cursing God and the king was a capital offence (Exod 22.28). Jezebel knew her Bible that well, but it did her little good.

The plan was to proclaim a fast, something which had to be justified perhaps because of a period of prolonged drought. Then, when the fast was beginning to bite, was the time to suggest that the reason for God's displeasure was that someone had sinned and done so grievously. With two witnesses to the deed and no one capable of denying it, Naboth had no defence to offer save his lifetime of good conduct. But the law was the law, and cursing God and the king was punishable by death by stoning, and only drastic measures would enable the fast to be lifted. So Naboth was condemned and put to death, and very likely (to judge from a later reference in 2 Kings 9.26) his sons were killed with him, thus ensuring that there were no other claimants to the property. Jezebel smiled in triumph. The vineyard was hers, to present to Ahab.

POETIC JUSTICE

She reckoned however without God's poetic justice. An overjoyed Ahab went straight to Samaria to take possession of his ill-gotten gain, but . . . 'the word of the Lord came to Elijah the Tishbite, saying, "Arise, go down to meet Ahab king of Israel, who is in Samaria . . . and you shall say to him, 'Thus says the Lord, "Have you killed and also taken possession? . . . In the place where dogs licked up the blood of Naboth shall dogs lick your own blood."' "'

You may say that that was small comfort to Naboth and his family. Could not the Lord have frustrated Jezebel's plan and stopped the kangaroo trial and saved Naboth's life? Yes, possibly he could. But God is not a God of constant interventions, or no sins would ever be committed, no people would die unjustly, no suffering would ever take place. He does not, however, leave injustice to triumph. He does bring villains to book, if not in time then certainly in eternity. Some years later, as the Bible story records, Elijah's words were fulfilled and the gruesome deaths of Ahab and Jezebel came about. Ahab died in battle with a modicum of honour; Jezebel was murdered appallingly with the same treachery she had shown to others. Justice had at last been done.

Before we leave the story, let us acknowledge the fourth character in the play, namely Elijah the prophet. He was incredibly brave to go and beard the lion Ahab in his newly-occupied den. If ever a man was in danger of his life, Elijah was that day. Tyrants hate those who challenge them and the more their consciences are stabbed the more wildly they lash out in return. It was after just such a meeting with the bestial Idi Amin that Archbishop Janani Luwum met his death. A martyrdom, if ever there was one.

Elijah got away with it. There must have been some trace of the fear of God in Ahab's Israelite heart that told him that Elijah was speaking the truth. Not his words but the word of the Lord, that would come true whether the speaker lived or died. He allowed him to state his unwelcome message: 'I have found you, because you have sold yourself to do what is evil in the sight of the Lord. I will bring evil upon you; I will utterly sweep you away . . . because you have made Israel to sin.'

No punches were pulled. And to our surprise Ahab rent his clothes, put sackcloth on himself as a sign of sorrow, fasted and, to quote Scripture, 'went about dejectedly'. No wonder. You could hardly credit him with a spirit of repentance, but he did show a degree of remorse and his sentence was lightened a little because of his show of humility. Yes, God can be gracious even to the most dastardly of people who commit the most horrifying crimes, but it was only a stay of execution. Eventually, and justly, the axe had to fall.

The story of Naboth and his vineyard is the archetypal one of the little man, the commoner, standing up for his rights against the power of a totalitarian state. Some of us would have preferred it to have been written differently, with the little man vindicated and the tyrant put down before he could work his will. But the Bible is realistic. It rarely happens like that. Power is powerful. Weakness is very weak. But we come away from the story knowing where God stands and that is reassuring, to say the least. And before we fail to notice it, just observe that the real power in the story is not Ahab's, nor Jezebel's nor Naboth's, nor even Elijah's, but it is the power of the word of the Lord. That is devastating power, and it speaks of justice and ensures that justice will one day triumph.

13
SUNDAY TRADING

Then I remonstrated with the nobles and said to them, 'What is this evil thing which you are doing, profaning the sabbath day?'

NEHEMIAH 13.17

Sunday trading has been a live issue for some time and continues to divide public opinion. There are no easy solutions. There is no common mind.

It was never plain sailing, even in Old Testament times. You would have thought that the fourth commandment settled the issue as far as Jews were concerned. 'Remember the sabbath day, to keep it holy. Six days shall you labour and do all your work; but the seventh day is a sabbath to the Lord your God; in it you shall not do any work . . .' But it was not as simple as that. What if your ox fell into a pit? Could you pull it out on the sabbath day? The answer was yes. But you were not to do the things you didn't have to do, the things that could wait until the next day. It was a precise religious embargo hedged about with reasonable extenuating circumstances.

SABBATH AND SUNDAY

Now no one is saying that the Christian Sunday is a carry-over from the Jewish Sabbath. The Sabbath was a day of rest to remind people that God rested on the seventh day after his work of creation. It was a calendared message that six days of work needed to be followed by one day of rest. Working without a break was destructive of the human spirit. Men and women, as well as society in general, needed a rhythm of rest following work.

59

Sunday, on the other hand, began life as a day of worship, celebrating the Resurrection and bringing Christians together in the early morning to pledge their loyalty to their Lord, irrespective of whether the day was a working day or a holiday. But it borrowed some of the Sabbath features, especially when it was structured into the life of the state by a Christian ruler like Constantine the Great. The point I am making is that you cannot argue straight from the Old Testament Sabbath to the Christian Sunday, for after all Jesus modified the Sabbath both by word and by example. He healed on the Sabbath; he performed miracles on the Sabbath; he defended his disciples picking a few ears of corn on the Sabbath and declared that the Sabbath was not an end in itself but a means to an end. 'The sabbath was made for man, not man for the sabbath.' Are we right then to look at a passage in the Book of Nehemiah and relate it to Sunday trading? Well, let us try.

We begin with Nehemiah himself. A man of great courage and character, he took on the powerful war-lords of the Persian empire and outwitted them. He oversaw the rebuilding of the walls of Jerusalem and gave the people back their respect and self-confidence. He was a man of action, but also of prayer. Every now and again he puts in a one-sentence prayer to keep himself attuned to God. An example to activists the world over.

He was a shrewd strategist as well. He knew where to concentrate his energies and he would not be deflected. He made good decisions and was a sound judge of character. He could spot a villain long before he ever showed his hand.

In chapter 13 of his memoirs he tells of a visit he made back to Babylon to report to the king who had originally sent him on his mission to Jerusalem. He was away a long time and when he returned to Jerusalem he found a sorry state of affairs. One of his chief antagonists had used his influence to take over part of the temple as his private apartment. Nehemiah threw out his furniture and sent him packing. The Levites, the temple personnel, had given up their work because no money was coming in for their upkeep and were having to fend for themselves on their own smallholdings. Nehemiah rounded them up, put them to work and saw to it that the tithes were paid in and that temple money was administered honestly. And there were the Sabbath traders.

WHAT WAS WRONG?

The first thing Nehemiah noticed was that out in the farms and vineyards men were working on the Sabbath. They were treading grapes, bringing in the harvest, loading up donkeys with produce and leading them into Jerusalem—all on the official day of rest. He could not stop them doing what they wanted to do on their own farms but as governor of Jerusalem he could control what happened in his own city. And when they sold their goods on the Sabbath, he issued them with a solemn warning.

But what was wrong with what they were doing? First, it was contrary to God's revealed will and word. Six days you shall work and on the seventh day you are to rest. Secondly, it affected other people and encouraged them to break the fourth commandment. You can't have people selling without having people buying as well. Thirdly, it affected others who did not take part either out of conviction or preference. They could not avoid the din and hubbub of street trading. The quality of their lives was being interfered with. Fourthly, it was an affront to the standards of the community which had been jealously guarded throughout the centuries of Israel's history. And fifthly, there was in Nehemiah's judgement good evidence for supposing that it was this same religious declension that had brought about the disaster of the Exile and the destruction of the temple over a century before. At any rate, that is what the prophets had said and they ought to know.

Nehemiah's warnings fell on deaf ears. The very next verse (13.16) tells how the city's fish merchants followed suit and brought in their goods to sell them on the Sabbath day. This time Nehemiah remonstrated with the nobles, the city fathers, who should have known better than to allow this kind of behaviour to go on under their very noses. The simple fact was that they looked the other way and let it happen regardless.

When warnings and protests failed, Nehemiah took action.

61

'When it began to be dark at the gates of Jerusalem before the sabbath, I commanded that the doors should be shut and gave orders that they should not be opened until after the sabbath.' That should have settled it once and for all but the merchants were nothing if not persistent. They responded by camping outside the city walls with their wares around them in the hope of enticing people to come out of the city and smuggle the goods inside. A little bribery was all that was needed, and nobody need be any the wiser. 'But I warned them', wrote Nehemiah, 'and said to them, "Why do you lodge before the wall? If you do so again I will lay hands on you."'

The threat of violence was reinforced by the stationing of guards at each of the city's gates, as the Levites were given the solemn task of purifying themselves to guard the gates and keep the sabbath day holy. It was enough to persuade the traders to melt away. They knew when they were beaten.

THE CURRENT DEBATE

Before we leave the story, what can we draw from it in relation to the current debate on the use of Sunday? First there is the religious dynamic. It was paramount for the Israelite because the law said quite specifically and unequivocally 'Thou shalt not'. It is less so for the Christian because Sunday's prime function is for worship as well as relaxation, and you cannot legislate to make worship compulsory. But if you believe that the first day of the week is a gift from God and for the worship of God—which is man's highest duty—you will defend its sanctity with more than casual concern. The Christian can never be neutral about the Lord's day.

Secondly, there is the profit-making dynamic. From earliest times the desire to profit from trade has led merchants to use every means at their disposal to sell their wares. They will cut corners, steal marches over their rivals, offer favours, bend the rules. They seem incapable of doing otherwise. And Nehemiah's traders were no exception. They were persistent to the last degree and only gave up when there was nothing further that they could do. Today's big stores are little different in their appetite for greater profits and a larger market-share. Often their very survival depends upon it. But then, as now, persistence has to be met with even greater persistence. Before Nehemiah came, the elders took the line of least resistance. He was made of sterner stuff and had the power as well as the determination to see them off the premises.

Thirdly, the weapons for the fight are prayer and action. If only one is used, there is little chance of success. But Nehemiah's resolute planning coupled with his arrow prayers to God won the day. He followed the dictum we often hear today:

> Work as if everything depends upon you,
> Pray as if everything depends upon God.

There are of course many more arguments which have been deployed in the debate over Sunday trading, to do with family life, the rights of workers and much besides. But Nehemiah's struggle has its place in the history of the preservation of the Lord's day and we admire him for the stand he took and the victory he achieved. May we be equally courageous in standing up for what is right.

14
RIGHT WITH GOD

Then Job answered: 'Truly I know that it is so; but how can a man be just before God?'

JOB 9.2

It was just after lunch on Sunday afternoon when the telephone rang. A woman's voice said 'Is that the Vicar? Father says would you come at once. He thinks he's going to die.' I knew who it was and that father was nearly 92. 'I'll be with you in ten minutes', I said and got into the car. I was the new vicar in a pair of Essex villages and had made it my aim to knock on every door, all five hundred of them, in my first month. I had just completed it, so I knew where the old man lived in the nearby hamlet and I drove there as fast as I could.

His daughter met me at the door. 'He knows he's dying, and he told me to ring you first, then the doctor. He wants to make his peace with God. He's very unhappy. Last night he dreamt that he had died and that God had accepted him. Then he woke up and realized that he hadn't.' I went upstairs to his room. He was conscious but the shallow breathing and the bluish lips gave out a warning that it might not be long. 'I want to make my peace with God', he said. I looked down at him on his low divan and replied 'You can't'. I nearly regretted saying it when I saw the look of blank dismay that came over him. Quickly I said 'You can't make your peace with God, because Christ has already made it for you'. Slowly understanding dawned as he realized there was nothing he needed to do to get right with God but only to rest his faith in what Jesus had done for him in dying on the cross for his sins.

We talked a while, then quietly he said after me the words of the old gospel hymn:

Jesus I do trust Thee, trust Thee with my soul;
Guilty, lost and helpless, Thou canst make me whole,
There is none in heaven or on earth like Thee,
Thou hast died for sinners; therefore, Lord, for me.

There are many, many people who share that old gentleman's longing to make his peace with God, to get right with him. Sometimes towards the end of their lives, but also when something about their life brings them up with a jolt. I once heard a man reciting a catalogue of his sins and at the end he asked me, almost as a challenge, 'Can God do anything for a man as bad as me?' I told him that he was just the sort of person God could do something for. Jesus said: 'I came not to call the righteous, but sinners to repentance.' You qualify!

JOB'S DILEMMA

In a way, it was Job's dilemma. 'How can a man (a mere man) be just before God?' How can a failure pass muster with a success? How can a sinner be acceptable to someone who is the personification of holiness and goodness? It is a question that has worried men's minds and consciences throughout time.

As far as Job was concerned, the question had an unusual twist to it. After all he *was* a good man, quite notoriously good. Even God thought so, as the opening chapter indicates. 'Have you considered my servant Job, that there is none like him on the earth, a blameless and upright man, who fears God and turns away from evil?' Job's problem was not that he was desperately conscious of his sinfulness but that everyone was telling him that the sufferings he had endured were due to his sins and he needed to repent of them before the Lord. So when he cried out in despair 'How can a man be just before God?', he was really asking how it was possible for an innocent man to prove his innocence before a God who allows him to suffer so grievously. Search his conscience as he might, he could unearth nothing that would merit the appalling succession of tragedies and disasters that he had had to live through.

His friends thought otherwise. You can hardly call them

comforters, because there was nothing comforting about their diagnosis of the problem. As far as they were concerned, the answer was obvious. Suffering followed sin, so the proper response to suffering was to repent in sackcloth and ashes. Do that, and the problem was solved. But of course, as Job saw it, that answer *was* the problem. The problem was not so much the suffering as the explanation of the suffering. The burden of the Book of Job is not the question of suffering but the inadequacy of orthodoxy, which Job's suffering highlighted. The book was a challenge to accepted beliefs, a protest against bad theology. What, if any, are the answers it comes up with?

REDEEMER

First, there was the answer that Job himself came out with in his memorable words: 'Though he slay me, yet will I trust in him' (13.15). Whatever God does to me or allows me to suffer, whatever cold comfort I am served up with by those who think they know better than I do, I am going to hang on to him and hope against hope that I shall be vindicated. Maybe not in this life. Maybe only after worms destroy this body. But one day I shall see God and he will be on my side. My Redeemer lives.

A second clue is to be found in the wrap-around part of the Book of Job, the introduction and conclusion in which the long poem is encased. Here the reader sees what Job himself never saw, namely, that God was using Job as a model of faithfulness to demonstrate to all and sundry that his godliness was not a fair-weather affair. 'Does Job fear God for naught?' asked the adversary. 'Yes, he certainly does', replied God, 'and I'll prove it to you.' Poor Job! If he had known this he might have made an even better showing, but of course the message is for us, the readers, in later generations. If we see suffering as a test-bed for our faith and as a witness to others, it makes it just that little bit easier to bear. But it will not make it go away.

The third shaft of light that the book sheds on Job's problem is to be found in the concluding speech of the Lord. Here God asks Job dozens of questions about the created world in order to remind Job how little he really knows and how far superior is God's understanding to his own. It is not a put-down. It is very gently done, but it has the desired effect. Job responds: 'I know that thou canst do all things, and that no purpose of thine can be thwarted . . . I had heard of thee by the hearing of the ear, but now my eye sees thee; therefore I despise myself, and repent in dust and ashes' (42.2–6).

COPING WITH SUFFERING

So the problem of suffering is never solved in Job, but then, as we have tried to show, suffering was not the problem. It was the faulty theology that surrounded it and tried to explain it all too glibly. Instead Job tells us how suffering may be coped with— with faith in an all-loving God, in humility before an all-knowing God, and in the hope that, bravely borne, it will in some way redound to his glory.

Which brings us back to our original question: How can a man be just before God? Or how can a dying man find his peace with God? The New Testament gives the answer that the Old can only hint at: through Jesus Christ our Lord. Through him we are justified. No, not forgiven; much more than that. We are justified, accounted righteous, accepted. Not for what we have done, because we are sinners and even our noblest acts are tainted with evil; but because of what Jesus Christ has done in his death and resurrection. As Paul put it in Romans 4.24–25, 'It (i.e. righteousness) will be reckoned to us who believe in him that raised from the dead Jesus our Lord, who was put to death for our trespasses and raised for our justification'. Through Christ we are acquitted before the judgement seat of God. Through Christ we do have peace with God, for he has made peace through the blood of his cross (Col 1.20), and so we can say with Paul (Romans again) 'Therefore, since we are justified by faith, we have peace with God through our Lord Jesus Christ. Through him we have obtained access to this grace in which we stand, and we rejoice in our hope of sharing the glory of God' (Rom 5.1–2).

Job was a long way from seeing New Testament truth, but he was on the right road. What is his persistent trust in God but the New Testament quality of saving faith? What is his vision of the greatness and wonder of God but the humble submission to his will that the New Testament asks of those who stand in his awesome presence? Our Lord called for his followers to have the trustfulness of a little child and the humility of a servant. Job showed those qualities out of the depths of his suffering. If by God's grace he could make it, so could we be just before God.

15
SOCIAL EVILS

Woe to those who draw iniquity with cords of falsehood, who draw sin as with cart ropes.

ISAIAH 5.18

From time to time I get the opportunity to visit the East of England Agricultural Show at Peterborough. While my wife prefers to look round the marquees of local crafts, my preference is to go to see the livestock, especially the cattle. They have been beautifully groomed, most unlike the cows you usually see in a field, but most impressive of all are the bulls. Huge specimens every one, that you would certainly not want to see in a field, not if you had to cross it, anyway. And yet they look incredibly docile and can be led around the arena by the stockman with nothing more than a hand-held rope through their nose-ring. Yet if they chose to object and to stand their ground, I doubt if any amount of tugging would budge their massive bulk.

It is this mental picture that I bring to today's text. The prophet Isaiah is writing about people who haul their wrongdoings about with them wherever they go. They are strangely attached to them, if not actually proud of them, and they drag them along as if they could not bear to be parted from them. They lead them by the nose, fondly imagining that they are in full control of them but never realizing that they are the servants and their sins at the end of the rope are their masters.

Isaiah is nothing if not specific in identifying some of his people's sins, and chapter 5 of his prophecy mentions no less than six evils that he introduces with the phrase 'Woe to those who . . .'. Let us have a look at some of them. They contain some surprising inclusions and some equally surprising omissions.

69

ACQUIRING LAND

'Woe to those who join house to house, who add field to field, until there is no more room, and you are made to dwell alone in the midst of the land' (verse 8). Now whatever is wrong with buying up the other half of your semi-detached and making them both into a pleasantly large villa? Or negotiating to buy the adjacent farm so that you can improve your holding of land? Why, I recall playing golf with a land agent in Southern Ireland who told me that his main job was to build up large estates for his clients by going to see small farmers and persuading them that it was worth their while to sell up and retire on the proceeds. And he was the pillar of his local church! Would he have come under the lash of Isaiah's tongue too? I am not sure, probably not.

What upset Isaiah, however, was the way in which the land was amassed and the social consequences that followed. In a country that held to a belief that the land belonged to God and was farmed by his tenants and not by private owners, there is little doubt that this verse refers to wealthy individuals acquiring land by dishonest means, through foreclosing on debts or forcing their less successful neighbours out of business. Such people were deaf to the law's demands that loans to fellow-Israelites should be interest-free and that land that changed hands had to revert to the original owner every seventh or every jubilee year.

What is more, the acquiring of large estates and many houses had undesirable social consequences. Rural communities were taken apart. The independence of yeoman farmers was being replaced by the need to kowtow to feudal landlords or their agents. Those who were displaced became an urban underclass as they migrated to the cities to find employment, often without success.

All this was 'Sin number one' in Isaiah's book: action which produced social disintegration. Surely, in our own day and in our own land, powerful individuals, corporations, local and national governments need to think very hard about their policies and the social consequences they bring in their train. Otherwise, they too will be condemned.

70

DRINKING TOO MUCH

This gets double treatment. In verse 11 we have 'Woe to those who rise early in the morning, that they may run after strong drink, who tarry late into the evening till wine inflames them!' And later, in verse 22, the prophet comes back to the subject with 'Woe to those who are heroes at drinking wine, and valiant men at mixing strong drink.'

We recognize them both only too well. The person who wakes up gasping for the first drink of the day is showing the classic sign of alcoholism and has a serious, deep-seated drink problem. The other man is the macho drinker, who is found in every club and in many a pub. His bombast is all about the pints he has downed, the bottles he has cracked, and he boasts that he can still walk down a straight white line and drive his car home. He thinks himself a hero. In truth he is an adolescent. He has never grown up.

The Bible is not against drink. It speaks of wine to gladden the heart of man, and the Lord Jesus used wine as the vehicle for the greatest sacramental symbol the world has known. But the Bible is full of warnings about its dangers. 'Wine is a mocker, strong drink a brawler; and whoever is led astray by it is not wise' (Prov 20.1). 'Do not get drunk with wine, for that is debauchery', writes Paul, 'but be filled with the Spirit' (Eph 5.18).

'Beware the demon Drink' was the watchword of the temperance societies of a century ago, and we smile indulgently at them from our more enlightened vantage-point. Maybe alcohol has given way to other drugs as the chief enemy of modern society, but it is still a powerful foe and is the cause of more broken lives and lost jobs than we care to admit. So Isaiah's words are not entirely without meaning for the world we live in today.

MORAL PERVERSITY

'Woe to those who call evil good and good evil, who put darkness for light and light for darkness, who put bitter for sweet and sweet for bitter!' (verse 20). I used to find it difficult to believe that people could turn morality on its head and misunderstand so completely standards of right and wrong.

71

How could they look at evil and call it good? How could they reject virtue in preference for vice? It seemed unbelievable that such a reversal of values could take place. But now I see how readily it can happen. All that is needed is a different frame of reference.

For instance, if you believe that your cause for, say, a united Ireland is the most important thing in the world to work for, then everything that will further that aim is good — in your eyes. Killing soldiers and policemen, leaving bombs in public places, causing havoc and slaughter, these are good things to do. The fact that innocent people are maimed and murdered, that children are orphaned and wives are widowed, is just an unfortunate but necessary result of the armed struggle against what you think to be tyranny. So, given the twisted moral logic by which you live, you can quite easily come to ethical judgements which are the very reverse of what most civilized men and women would hold to.

Now, you don't have to be a member of the Provisional IRA for Isaiah's cap to fit. Almost any frame of reference that is distinctly different from the Judaeo-Christian one can lead you into the trap. Regard human life as something less than sacred and you can treat some people as expendable, fit for the incinerator or the gas-chamber. Believe yourself to be the only person who really counts and you will manipulate and trample your way through life in order to make it to the top.

Woe to people who live like that, said Isaiah. They will not get to the top at all. They will be brought low and called to account—one day. They are like people who are 'wise in their own eyes, and shrewd in their own sight' (verse 21), but the only eyes that matter are God's eyes and he sees our foolishness for what it is. And he will be our judge.

OMISSIONS

I have no idea why Isaiah, the great prophet of eighth-century Israel, picked on these three evils as the ones he wanted to preach against. Why not sexual immorality, for it certainly abounded at the time? Why not dishonesty or robbery with violence, or oppression? We cannot say. But these dire warnings were uttered because at the time he felt them to be the crucial issues of the day. Our social evils may be the same. They may be different. But there are some meeting-points between Isaiah's day and ours.

First, we too must be aware of any influence at work in our nation that leads to the kind of social disintegration that he could see around him as a result of changes in rural life and private ownership. Secondly, we must be on our guard against the intoxicating influences that warp our judgement, deaden our faculties, lower our self-respect and take away our manliness. And finally, we are challenged to hold fast to a truly Christian world-view, so that our moral barometer is accurate and our ethical decisions are sound.

We may think that we have taken a good look at Isaiah's chapter of 'woes' in this sermon, and it is quite true that every one of those mentioned in chapter 5 has been touched on, at the very least. But there is one more to come. In the following chapter, Isaiah tells of his vision in the temple, where he saw the Lord, high and lifted up, in all his glory; and the seraphim were singing of his holiness and splendour. And before that holy Lord God of hosts, the prophet found himself bowing in humble adoration and in penitence, saying, 'Woe is me! For I am lost; for I am a man of unclean lips, and I dwell in the midst of a people of unclean lips; for my eyes have seen the King, the Lord of hosts!'

It is no accident that after a succession of woes directed at other people, Isaiah comes to the point of saying 'Woe is me'. Yes, if I am going to set myself up as judge of other people's wrongdoings, I must first begin with myself and my own sinfulness, for I too hold the end of a rope in my hand. And behind me I trail my sins which hold me back and are a constant burden to me. I need to bring them in penitence to the cross and, kneeling there, to let go of the rope. Only then will I be delivered from their mastery and I shall become truly free.

16
OFF WITH THE YOKE

Is not this the fast that I choose: to loose the bonds of wickedness, to undo the thongs of the yoke, to let the oppressed go free, and to break every yoke?

ISAIAH 58.6

I was walking through the streets of Norwich some time ago and found myself passing the Salvation Army citadel. Outside was a large poster with the words 'Self-Denial Week: Come and hear the Citadel Band'. I felt it could have been better worded.

Undoubtedly the Salvation Army has put us all in its debt by its insistence on keeping to self-denial every Lent and urging others to do the same. We are not very good at Lenten discipline, or any other kind of discipline for that matter, as evidenced by the hopeless way in which we make the occasional pretence of dieting to do away with unwanted flab. The truth is that it is not at all easy to diet when others are eating without inhibition, and it is much easier when it is done collectively. That was the merit of fast-days which were kept by the whole community, as was done in ancient Israel, as well as by present-day Jews.

The 58th chapter of Isaiah deals with the all-important question of fasting, but the prophet is critical if not downright contemptuous of the way it was being practised. 'Fasting like yours this day', he wrote, 'will not make your voice to be heard on high. Is such the fast that I choose, a day for a man to humble himself? Is it to bow down his head like a rush, and to spread sackcloth and ashes under him? Will you call this a fast, and a day acceptable to the Lord?' (verses 4b–5).

Fasting of this kind clearly will not do. The prophet explains why. 'Behold, in the day of your fast you pursue your own business, and oppress all your workers. Behold, you fast only to quarrel and to fight and to hit with wicked fist.' In other words, fasting is only acceptable if it is accompanied by good business practice and the forsaking of threatening and oppressive behaviour. Righteous conduct is as good as fasting any day.

UNDOING

For some reason the word 'yoke' plays an important part in the prophet's thinking at this stage. He refers to it three times. First he talks about undoing the thongs of the yoke (verse 6), then to breaking every yoke (6b) and finally to taking away the yoke (9). The word he uses is the common word for a pole or staff, like those used to carry the ark of the Lord, but then it comes to mean the cross-bar which is laid upon the shoulders of a pair of oxen yoked to a plough or the pole carried by a burden-bearer to balance two heavy loads that he is carrying. The thongs suggest the harness with which it was attached to the animals or maybe to the carrier.

The picture is a vivid one. The yoke is the oppressive burden placed upon hard-working and often weary shoulders, and the prophet demands that this should be eased and the thongs that hold it in place should be untied, so that the oppressed can go free. He then goes further and urges that the yoke should be broken in two so that it can never be used again, and that the freedom should be permanent. Then finally he demands that the yoke as a symbol of the imposition of unfair burdens on the weakest in society should be done away with once and for all.

This has a startling relevance to some of today's social conditions. There is nothing wrong with carrying burdens. Many of us choose to do so or willingly undertake them for the sake of our families or our livelihood. The social evil is when men and women are ground down by conditions that they have not accepted freely for themselves but are imposed upon them by others or by the circumstances of their daily lives. For them life is a kind of imprisonment: a constant, unrelenting and inescapable bondage from which they see little chance of freeing themselves. Those in the so-called poverty trap are a case in point. More particularly, this applies to those countless people who are crushed under the burden of spiralling debt. And they are not by any means the victims of their own mismanagement. Redundancy, sickness, a new baby that prevents the mother from bringing in an extra income, all these conspire to turn a mortgage into a nightmare. With the threat of dispossession from the family home a young couple and their children face an appallingly bleak future saddled with a debt they see no prospect of paying off and with their once secure life shattered and degraded. A yoke indeed—and what are *we* doing to help unloose those thongs?

SHARING

The call to those who have is to share—their bread with the hungry, their homes with the homeless, their clothing with the destitute. Yet there is something in our Western way of life that baulks at obeying this command too literally. We have no objection to making a donation or paying a subscription but we prefer it to be done from a safe distance. We value the space between ourselves and the recipients of our charity. We prefer others to administer our giving, because we do not want to get involved with the needy ourselves.

Maybe it has to do with the old saying about the Englishman's home being his castle. It needs ramparts and a drawbridge to guarantee our own security. Few of us can allow our inner family sanctum to be invaded by strangers. We jealously protect our privacy. It seems to reflect a basic human need in our society, perhaps because the extended family is a thing of the past and the barriers around our small nuclear families have had to be drawn more tightly. A large household is more capable of welcoming in the occasional stray visitor than the small, semi-detached family unit we are accustomed to. We should not feel guilty about this. Our times are not the same as they were in Old Testament days. We cannot give hospitality to all the waifs and strays in town, or take in everyone who is sleeping rough.

But we must share more. And the people who must head the

list of those we need to help are the hungry, the homeless and the destitute. Thank God that Christian consciences are slowly being awoken to this need and in many towns and cities there are now initiatives to assist in providing food, clothing and shelter for those who otherwise would be sleeping rough in doorways and public parks. And yet we are still incredibly slow in responding to their needs. We still have our cardboard cities and have not yet been shamed by them into adequate response. We make an effort for a few days with the annual 'Crisis at Christmas' appeal, but then enthusiasm wanes and the needy are left to fend for themselves. Wasn't it Ebenezer Scrooge who said 'Are there no prisons, and the Union workhouses, are they still in operation? Those who are badly off must go there. It's not my business'? And the voice of Scrooge leaving the problem to the state or to others can still be heard in the land, sometimes from within our own hearts. Yet we cannot close our eyes to the problems that still exist around us. We must share more of what we have with those who have little or nothing. Otherwise, how can we live with ourselves and our consciences?

POURING

Verse 9 invites the prophet's hearers not only to remove the yoke from their midst but also to get rid of 'the pointing of the finger, and speaking wickedness' and to pour themselves out for the hungry and satisfy the desire of the afflicted. Pointing the finger was a gesture of derision. It is still practised with evident malicious delight by the political activists and campaigners and protesters who are nightly shown on our television screens. Behind the rhetoric there is the voice of anger and bitterness too. But what, I wonder, does it do to our society when we give vent to the language and gestures of derision and contempt for our fellow-men and women? When the health of our community is dependent on mutual respect, and the principles of democracy teach us to disagree without violence, why do we allow ourselves to be tempted into the inflammatory and contemptuous words and actions which are guaranteed to prove destructive? It might be helpful if the House of Commons were to set a better example to the rest of us in this regard.

The apostle Paul thought of himself as being 'poured as a libation upon the sacrificial offering of your faith', when he wrote to the Christians in Philippi (Phil 2.17), and it is this quality of self-giving, being poured out, that our text from Isaiah 58 urges upon us. 'If you pour yourself out for the hungry' means that you sacrifice your life in meeting their needs. You can hardly have a stronger metaphor. It reminds one of Our Lord's language when he said that 'the Son of man came not to be ministered unto but to minister and to give his life as a ransom for many'. Or again, 'Greater love has no man than this, that a man lay down his life for his friends'. This self-emptying, being poured out, is like the ultimate sacrifice, when nothing is held back, all is given away.

What then do we do? Sell all that we have and give it to the poor? The standard set before us is impossibly high, but we need to have the ultimate in our sights so that we are spurred on towards a greater degree of generosity and self-giving ourselves.

REWARDS

There is a promised reward as the incentive to strive for a more just and compassionate society. 'The Lord will guide you continually, and satisfy your desire with good things, and make your bones strong; and you shall be like a watered garden, like a spring of water, whose waters fail not.' Yes, there is a recompense for those who pour themselves out in love and service. Not emptiness but abundance. Not being drained but being replenished. Not resources reduced, but a spring of water that never fails. We have Our Lord's words for it: 'Out of his heart shall flow rivers of living water.' The people who truly give, give of themselves, will discover an inner satisfaction; they will find they have yet more to give.

17
NO JUSTICE

The Lord saw it, and it displeased him that there was no justice.

ISAIAH 59.15

'There's no justice', we say, when someone who hasn't done a hand's turn to deserve it gets showered with good fortune, and we get nothing at all. Usually we say it with a bit of a smile, but underneath there is just a touch of resentment or disappointment. And the truth is that there often *is* no justice in life. The rain falls upon the just and the unjust, but the sun seems to shine only on the unrighteous. At any rate that's what it feels like.

Isaiah's words, however, tell a much deeper story. He was not complaining about the minor injustices of life but about the almost total lack of integrity among the people of his day. It showed itself in a hundred different ways. Try to get an impartial hearing in the courts and you were doomed to failure. 'No one enters suit justly, no one goes to law honestly; they rely on empty pleas, they speak lies, they conceive mischief and bring forth iniquity' (Isa 59.4). Standards in public life have sunk to an all-time low and local politics have become hopelessly corrupt. 'Truth has fallen in the public squares, and uprightness cannot enter' (59.14). Violence stalks the streets; protection rackets abound; private vendettas go unchecked. 'Deeds of violence are in their hands. Their feet run to evil, and they make haste to shed innocent blood' (59.6–7).

This makes for a pretty depressing scenario and we wonder what a prophet can make of it, apart, that is, from simply denouncing it and issuing threats against those who make it so. We often feel that we are up against a similarly intractable problem of social disorder and we feel powerless to know what to do. Indeed, is there anything that anyone can do except pray and feel miserable? Well, let us listen to Isaiah's analysis of the situation in the 59th chapter of his book, and see if any light is shed on the problem.

SEPARATION FROM GOD

Isaiah begins the chapter in a positive, optimistic mood. 'The Lord's hand is not shortened, that it cannot save, or his ear dull, that it cannot hear; but your iniquities have made a separation between you and your God, and your sins have hid his face from you so that he does not hear' (verses 1–2). Clearly someone has come up to the prophet and asked him why God isn't answering their prayers and doing something about it. And his answer is that God is quite capable of dealing with the situation but it needs to be understood as a spiritual issue and not purely as a social or political problem. The nation's sins have produced an enormous gap between the people and the Lord, and that is where the solution needs first to be found.

There is a difficulty here which you may have noticed. How can it be said that God does not *hear* people's prayers? Surely he hears and sees everything. Should the prophet not have said that because of the people's sins, the Lord will hear but will not choose to answer? That would probably be our way of putting things. But in Hebrew the word for 'to hear' represents not simply the impact of a voice upon the ear-drum, but also the response to that voice in some sort of action. So when the Old Testament says that God hears the prayers of his people, it means that he does something in response to them. 'To hear' does in fact imply 'to answer'. But Isaiah is clear that there will be no favourable answer from God as long as the people's sins are separating them from him. He may hear our prayers but the response is nil.

LOOKING FOR JUSTICE

Verses 9–15 indicate a change of mood. Before that, the writer is

80

talking about what *they* do. The villains, the violent, the crooks and the con-men. But now he changes to the first person plural. 'We look for light, and behold, darkness, and for brightness, but we walk in gloom. We grope for the wall like the blind . . . we stumble at noon as in the twilight . . . we look for justice, but there is none; for salvation, but it is far from us.'

Then he identifies himself with his people's sins. 'Our transgressions are multiplied before thee, and our sins testify against us; for our transgressions are with us, and we know our iniquities.' What a transformation! No longer *their* sins, destroying the nation and corrupting its life, but *ours*, cutting us off from God's mercy and making him deaf to all our pleas. Repentance starts here—in the Church and most of all in me.

IS ANYONE THERE?

The next section of the chapter begins with the words of our text. 'The Lord saw it, and it displeased him that there was no justice', and it continues, 'He saw that there was no man and wondered that there was no one to intervene'. It was not the first time that God was on the look-out for just one person to stand in the breach and serve him in a difficult situation.

In the course of Isaiah's vision the voice of the Lord said 'Whom shall I send, and who will go for us?' And many, many times in Christian history God has called for volunteers to come out and offer themselves for his service. It is not a great army he requires. He wants picked men and women. One here, one there. They must be willing to stand out against the crowd, and to be totally committed to their Lord and to his cause. We note with shame that in our text God's call went out in vain. There was no one to intervene. No volunteers.

HE COMES IN PERSON

So God's own messenger was sent. 'His own arm brought him

81

victory, and his righteousness upheld him. He put on righteousness as a breastplate, and a helmet of salvation upon his head; he put on garments of vengeance for clothing, and wrapped himself in fury as a mantle' (verses 16–17). It is the familiar theme of God's personal intervention when all his people have failed him. And it is of course the message of the Christian gospel.

'God has done what the law, weakened by the flesh, could not do', wrote Paul to the Romans. 'Sending his own Son in the likeness of sinful flesh and for sin, he condemned sin in the flesh, in order that the just requirement of the law might be fulfilled in us, who walk not according to the flesh but according to the Spirit' (Rom 8.3–4). Or, as St Luke put it in the song of Zechariah, John the Baptist's father: 'Blessed be the Lord God of Israel, for he has visited and redeemed his people' (Luke 1.68).

Yes, God has done it himself. He has come in the person of his Son, Jesus Christ Our Lord, as Isaiah promised and predicted, to ensure that one day there would be justice, there would be someone to intervene. And so it is that through Christ's death the gulf that separates man from God has been bridged. The victory has been won.

We cannot leave this passage without noting its similarity to the Christian's armour in Ephesians 6. The breastplate of righteousness and the helmet of salvation are consciously borrowed by St Paul, with the shield of faith and the sword of the Spirit added, to make the equipment God provides for the Christian battlefield. Unlike Saul's armour, which was many sizes too large for David to wear in his challenge to Goliath, God's armour fits us exactly and corresponds precisely to our needs. It is after all the equipment with which he won the battle himself.

Occasionally you see by the side of a road an abandoned car on the grass verge. Your natural instinct is to wonder if it is stolen and to inform the police. But now the local constabulary have had to deal with the excessive helpfulness of the public and so, until they can trace the owner or get the car towed away, you will find a notice stuck on the windscreen with the two words 'Police Aware'. It means you needn't worry them; they know.

The message of Isaiah 59 to those who are worried and discouraged by the darkness and wrongdoing that press in upon every side is just this: God is aware. He knows and he has a plan to put things right. But be warned. It could be that he is looking for you to help.

18
DROP THE DEAD DONKEY

*With the burial of an ass he shall be buried, dragged and cast forth
beyond the gates of Jerusalem.*

JEREMIAH 22.19

This is hardly the language you ought to use about your king,
but if you knew Jeremiah you would understand. And if you
knew who he was speaking about, you would understand even
better. The man's name was Jehoiakim, king of Judah, and he
and the prophet Jeremiah were sworn enemies most of the time.
Let me tell you what I know about him.

For a start, Jehoiakim was not his real name; it was Eliakim.
He was put on the throne in Jerusalem by the king of Egypt, who
was for a few brief years the most powerful man in the Middle
East. He wanted a safe man in his neighbouring kingdom so he
ousted Jehoahaz from the throne and replaced him with his
brother Eliakim. But he changed his name to incorporate the
name of Israel's God, Yahweh, to give the impression that he
was Yahweh's man, Jehoiakim, meaning 'The Lord has
established it'. It was a long way from the truth, and Jeremiah
had some devastating things to say about him in chapter 22,
verses 13–19.

HIS PLUSH PALACE

His opening words were 'Woe to him who builds his house by
unrighteousness, and his upper rooms by injustice;. . . who says,
"I will build myself a great house with spacious upper rooms",
and cuts out windows for it, panelling it with cedar, and painting
it with vermilion' (verses 13–14). It was not as if he hadn't got a
perfectly good palace in Jerusalem to live in. It had been more

84

than adequate for his father, Josiah, who had concentrated his attention on restoring the Lord's temple. But Jehoiakim's priorities were different. He planned to extend, to beautify and to impress his people with the splendour of the royal court. That was where he put his energies to work.

There can surely be nothing intrinsically wrong in restoring an ancient building or in collecting works of art or in employing skilled craftsmen to decorate and enlarge a dwelling. Visit Hatfield House or Woburn Abbey or Luton Hoo in my diocese and you will see breathtaking splendour in these historic houses, and it is gratifying that so many thousands of visitors can look round them every year and be uplifted by what they see. In every case, this is to the credit of a previous owner who set out to make his house a place of splendour and of his descendants who have struggled to maintain it for future generations to enjoy.

When we go round these historic homes with guidebook in hand, we are rarely in a position to judge whether the wealth used was well earned or not. In Jehoakim's case it was definitely not. Jeremiah accuses him not only of arrogant pride in choosing to lavish so much on himself but also of injustice in the way he acquired his possessions. He 'builds his house by unrighteousness'.

SWEATED LABOUR

The only hint we have of the nature of the king's injustice is in the phrase that follows: 'Who makes his neighbour serve him for nothing, and does not give him his wages.' It was a familiar story among some Old Testament kings. They had the power to exact forced labour from their people, and they exercised it all too often and for the wrong reasons. Solomon had done it with slave labour and had then forced it upon his own citizens. For all his greatness and the impressive achievements of his reign, they had been won at the cost of public goodwill. And now, three hundred years later, Jehoiakim was going down this well-trodden path.

Notice how Jeremiah puts it. He 'makes his *neighbour* serve him for nothing'. This miserable, imposed-upon work-force were the king's 'neighbours', his own compatriots, who should have been able freely to rub shoulders with him in the community of God's free people. Instead their rights were taken away, and for part of the year at any rate they were obliged to take part in what was called 'community service', but all that meant was building ever more splendid additions to the royal palace. And if there was any prospect or expectation of receiving payment for their labours, as was every citizen's right, it turned out to be a vain hope. No money; only the reply 'You're lucky to have work to do'. There would have been times when they would not have complained. Times of danger or stringency or national emergency. But this was just to satisfy a monarch's inordinate lust for power and prestige. Injustice indeed!

SO UNLIKE HIS FATHER

Jeremiah puts the boot in and asks 'Do you think you are a king because you compete in cedar?' (verse 15). The man who tries to justify his position by being competitive, particularly in such matters as the kind of house he lives in, is only demonstrating his insecurity and unfitness to be a king. Real kings don't need to prove it.

This raises an important point. Why do we compete so strenuously with each other? What are we trying to prove? What is it in the human heart that is always striving to excel? Is it because we are not sure of ourselves or our status, and therefore we feel we must go one better than anyone else? Is this the psychology behind keeping up with the Joneses? It is a far cry from the apostle Paul, who wrote 'I have learned, in whatever state I am, to be content' (Phil 4.11). Or again, 'There is great gain in godliness with contentment' (1 Tim 6.6). Jehoiakim would have scored few marks in the apostle's book.

Jeremiah goes on to compare Jehoiakim with his father. Josiah had been such a good king, and his long and godly reign had ushered in a spiritual revival which was to be remembered for centuries to come. How strange it is that his sons should not have followed in his footsteps. 'Did not your father eat and drink and do justice and righteousness? Then it was well with him. He judged the cause of the poor and needy; then it was well' (verses 15–16). Josiah was in fact the copybook king. Everything that could reasonably be expected of a good king, he had complied with. Rooting out idolatry, restoring the temple, reinstating the book of the law, revising his behaviour according to its precepts. He was everything that the prophets of the Lord could have wished for. But not Jehoiakim. He aspired to his father's greatness without having the slightest idea how to achieve it. So the prophet's indictment comes: 'You have eyes and heart only for your dishonest gain, for shedding innocent blood, and for practising oppression and violence' (verse 17).

It was not difficult to produce chapter and verse for Jehoiakim's atrocities. Quite apart from his treatment of Jeremiah, there had been the appalling scandal of what he had done to another prophet named Uriah. He too had prophesied in language similar to Jeremiah's and like Jeremiah had earned the king's disapproval. Jehoiakim must have been so stung by his words that he sentenced him to death, and when the frightened Uriah fled to Egypt to escape his fate, Jehoiakim sent an assassination squad to capture him and bring him back to face execution.

DEAF TO GOD'S WORD

Uriah's death well illustrated Jehoiakim's determination not to be subject to outside criticism, and certainly not from his puritanical father's God or one of that God's prophets. One of the most vivid stories Jeremiah tells us is to be found in chapter 36, where the words of his prophecies, painstakingly dictated to his secretary Baruch, are read to the king and his princes. The king was sitting in his winter quarters and a brazier was burning in front of him. As each section of the scroll was read out to the king, he cut it off with a penknife and threw it into the fire until every word had been read and the scroll was totally destroyed.

The story tells us much about Jehoiakim. He wanted to hear the word of the Lord through Jeremiah but he was determined to silence it before it did any damage. He is not the only person who has found that God's word has a fascination that makes it compulsory listening, but at the same time packs a challenge which it is more comfortable to avoid. The truth is, however, that the word cannot be silenced. It lives on in the conscience and memory. It goes on striving to gain admittance to the human heart. It will not go away. It does little good to extinguish the messenger; he will only be replaced by someone else. Or to destroy the book; Jeremiah promptly dictated a second one, longer than the first!

There was always the possibility—and no doubt it was Jeremiah's frequent prayer—that eventually Jehoiakim would turn to follow in the ways of his father, but the Bible gives no record of that conversion ever taking place. All we have are the words of our text, as Jeremiah utters the final condemnation of such unprincipled behaviour on the part of the one who had been called to be 'the shepherd of Israel'. 'With the burial of an ass he shall be buried, dragged and cast forth beyond the gates of Jerusalem.'

History does not confirm the fulfilment of that prediction. The only reference to Jehoiakim's death says that after doing what was evil in the sight of the Lord, he 'slept with his fathers'. But he was only 36 years of age and it would be very surprising if his death was from natural causes. Maybe Jeremiah's words came true. Maybe they were a warning that also constituted a call to repentance. We shall never know. But in this stubborn man, deaf to the word of God, blind to the secret of his father's greatness, resistant to criticism and motivated only by a desire for splendour and self-advancement at whatever cost to others, we have a chilling portrait of warning to us all. Though we would not have wished it on him, an ass's burial would have been a fitting end.

19
A LONG WAY FROM HOME

Seek the welfare of the city where I have sent you into exile, and pray to the Lord on its behalf, for in its welfare you will find your welfare.

JEREMIAH 29.7

Among the personal effects that came down to me after my mother's death was a letter. It had been in the family for years and no one was able to tell me how it came to be there. It was written to a minister in Northumberland and it was signed by none other than Grace Darling. The name means very little to this generation but to our grandparents she was a national heroine. The story of her courage, as a lighthouse keeper's daughter, in rowing out with her father to save nine shipwrecked survivors clinging to rocks in the Farne Islands was one of the legends of early Victorian England. Now, 150 years later, she is remembered only in the Grace Darling Museum in Bamburgh.

Tantalizingly, the letter tells us very little. It reflects her modesty and her faith, but is valuable chiefly for her signature. We would want to ask all sorts of questions of her and her correspondent. What kind of letter was she answering? Was the recipient a special friend or just one of her innumerable admirers? An isolated letter from the past leaves so many questions unanswered.

So it is with Jeremiah's letter from which our text is a quotation. We know when it was written—soon after the Exile had begun in 597 BC. We know who it was sent to—the people of Judah exiled in Babylon and daily wondering when they would be allowed to return home. We know how it reached them—by the hand of a small delegation being sent to Nebuchadnezzar to assure him that King Zedekiah was still loyal to him. Beyond that there has to be a certain amount of guesswork.

First and foremost, we must be on our guard against applying to others what Jeremiah had to say to his compatriots in exile. We cannot read off from Jeremiah 29 how political exiles are to behave today, nor hostages, nor people imprisoned under an oppressive regime. But we can and should learn from the way in which the prophet advised his readers, as they faced their own, unique ordeal.

FACE THE FACTS

The letter begins with the words 'Thus says the Lord of hosts, the God of Israel, to all the exiles whom I have sent into exile from Jerusalem to Babylon'. They may have thought that fate was against them or that their captivity was just one of the misfortunes of war, but Jeremiah said that it was their own God who had sent them into exile. He had intended it, and the sooner they accepted the fact the better.

There are some offenders who are notoriously unwilling to accept the reality of the crimes they have committed. They pass them off as 'technical offences', or excuse themselves by saying that everyone does these things and it was just bad luck that they were caught. Maybe so, but facing up to the facts is usually one of the surest ways to grow from guilt to grace. And what are guilt and punishment but our conscience's way and society's way of leading us from wrongdoing to righteousness? So don't, says Jeremiah, wallow in self-pity or dream idly of the day when you will be back home in your beloved Jerusalem, because you are going to be away for a long, long time.

Facing the facts, however unpalatable, means acting accordingly. So the exiles were advised to 'Build houses and live in them; plant gardens and eat their produce. Take wives and have sons and daughters; take wives for your sons, and give your daughters in marriage, that they may bear sons and daughters; multiply there, and do not decrease.' In other words, prepare for a lifelong stay in Babylon and settle down.

Meanwhile other prophets were giving a different message. They were promising the exiles that the Lord would not allow Jerusalem to disappear but that in a very few years he would see to it that they would be allowed home and would re-establish Jerusalem as the Lord's own city in the Lord's own land. Jeremiah accused them of prophesying lies. He said they were guilty of glossing over Israel's sins instead of taking them seriously. Prophets do not always say the same thing. Prophecies need to be heard critically.

Much the same division of opinion occurred in the Holy Land at the time of the Arab–Israeli War of 1947. The Arabs who were dispossessed from their homes in Palestine and sought refuge in Jericho and Gaza were torn between two paths: whether to seek to be assimilated into the life of Jordan and make their own way in life as stateless Palestinians, or to herd together in the tented camps supplied by the United Nations and prepare for the day when they could drive the Jews out of Israel and return to what they believed was their rightful home. Thus was the Palestine Liberation Organization born, and everyone knows how hard it has been for aspirations to be redirected and a reconciliation achieved.

I am not saying whose policy was right. The plain fact is that there was no possibility that all the refugees could have been absorbed. All I am saying is that Israel was faced with the same dilemma in 597 BC as the Palestinian Arabs were in AD 1947. To resist or to settle down.

Jeremiah advocated a 'settle down' policy. House-building and not shanty towns. Gardens and vineyards instead of uncultivated dereliction. Family life and not a festering sore.

SAY YOUR PRAYERS

Alongside these practical and domestic matters, the exiles were urged to take a positive spiritual stance in praying for the city where they lived and for the people who were their captors. It seems clear from other sources that they were not held in tight prison security. More likely it was in fairly open internment camps or reservations, where they had limited freedom to order their own affairs. Security was provided by the 600 miles of desert sand that separated them from their homeland.

There they were urged to begin praying for the Babylonians, their sworn enemies. In writing those words, Jeremiah was breaking new ground. It was to be another 600 years before 'love your enemies' was going to be taught, and even now, 2,000 years on, this still goes against the grain for many people. Jeremiah appealed to self-interest. 'In their welfare you will find your welfare.' There was not necessarily any merit in praying for Babylonians just because they were Babylonians, or in praying for their conversion because they had behaved so cruelly to them. They were to be prayed for on the basis of their welfare, literally, 'their peace', because if they were in good heart and prospering, it would be easier for the exiles to tolerate living in their midst. It was only a small step on the way to loving your enemies, but it was a step in the right direction.

SEEK THE LORD

It was one thing to pray to the Lord but quite another thing to expect him to hear or to be near at hand. After all, like all good Israelites, the exiles believed that his dwelling-place was at Jerusalem and that he was not to be found in the God-forsaken parts where they now dwelt. So yet another barrier needed to be negotiated if Jeremiah was going to introduce them to the idea that the Lord was God of the whole world and could be found in Babylon as well as in Jerusalem, To most of them it seemed to be quite a new idea, in spite of the many earlier hints that the God of Israel was much more than their own private tribal deity. Had not Isaiah's vision been of the Lord God of hosts and the whole earth was full of his glory? And had not the patriarchs experienced God at every stage of their travels, from Ur of the Chaldeans to Egypt and then into the promised land?

Jeremiah assured them that the Lord *was* with them. He could be prayed to and would hear. But on one condition: they must seek him with their whole heart. 'Then you will call upon me and come and pray to me, and I will hear you. You will seek me and find me; when you seek me with all your heart, I will be found by you, says the Lord' (verses 12–14). Casualness in religion is of no value at all. God does not respond to curiosity or to idle enquiry. The only way to find him is through being a committed seeker. 'Ask, seek, knock' is the triple thrust of Jesus' invitation. The dilettante will seek and will not find. The person who is burdened with the weight of his sin and guilt will seek in desperation, and for him success is assured. But not for everyone. The one thing the exiles could be sure of was that geography had nothing to do with it. The Lord could be found anywhere, even by the waters of Babylon.

REMEMBER ZION

Mention of the waters of Babylon calls to mind that hauntingly beautiful Psalm 137:

> By the waters of Babylon, there we sat down and wept,
> when we remembered Zion.
> On the willows there we hung up our lyres.
> For there our captors required of us songs, and our
> tormentors, mirth, saying,
> 'Sing us one of the songs of Zion!'
> How shall we sing the Lord's song in a foreign land?
> If I forget you, O Jerusalem, let my right hand wither!

Jeremiah would not have disagreed. He was not advocating a wholesale forgetfulness of the past in the interests of settling down to a long stay in exile. It was only right and proper that Jerusalem should continue to be their highest joy. There was a sense in which the exiles would be in mourning for their homeland as long as they were parted from it. Yes, let them sing to each other the songs of Zion but keep them from their captors' ears. They were too sacred to be thus debased and secularized.

There is no contradiction between remembering and settling down. To build houses does not mean that we forget that 'here we have no lasting city, but we seek the city which is to come' (Heb 13.14). Praying for the world we live in does not imply

93

that we have succumbed to worldliness. We must always remember.

Remember the Lord who brought you out of the house of bondage, out of the land of Egypt. Remember the rock from which you have been hewn. Remember the redemption that has been won for you by Christ on Calvary. Do this in remembrance of him; and look forward to the day when you eat and drink in his eternal presence.

Meanwhile, live this life to his glory, even though you are a long way from home.

20

MR RIGHTEOUS

The steadfast love of the Lord never ceases, his mercies never come to an end; they are new every morning; great is thy faithfulness.

LAMENTATIONS 3.22

One of the greatest days in my annual diary is Maundy Thursday. For that is the day when I have to attend the Queen at the service of the Royal Maundy. As Lord High Almoner (a somewhat Gilbertian title) it is my duty to arrange the service in a different cathedral each year and to stand alongside the Queen as she gives the red and white purses containing the silver Maundy money to the elderly recipients. As you can imagine, it is a very moving occasion but for me there is nothing quite so spine-tingling as the moment when the Chapel Royal choir begins to sing Handel's beautiful anthem 'Zadok the Priest', culminating in its repeated cry, 'God save the king, long live the king'. It is enough to set the whole place alight.

But who was Zadok and what did he do to merit being set to music? In the Old Testament, he was probably the most influential priest in King David's court in Jerusalem, and with Nathan the prophet he was responsible for the coronation of Solomon as David's successor. Hence his place in Handel's coronation anthem.

What interests me, however, is his name, Zadok, meaning 'righteous'. Fancy being called Mr Righteous! What a name to have to live up to. I always feel sorry for children who are given virtuous-sounding Christian names that they may not be able to exemplify. Names like Charity, Faith or even Christian. Fortunately Zadok was righteous. He lived out justice and loyalty and was rewarded by being the forerunner of a long line of high priests in ancient Israel.

GOING STRAIGHT

Hebrew has a number of words associated with the idea of justice and *zedeq* is one. It is translated either 'righteousness' or 'justice' and one of its adjectives is *zadoq*. In origin it means 'to be straight', like a plumb-line. Then it comes to mean conforming to a norm, and so from there to the qualities we associate with the word 'righteous'. The 'paths of righteousness for his name's sake' that we sing about in the 23rd Psalm are really 'straight paths' along which we ask God to lead us. If we stray from these paths we go wrong and fall into sin.

God is a God of righteousness. He is utterly straight and undevious. He is described in the letter of James as 'the Father of lights with whom there is no variableness, neither shadow of turning' (James 1.17 KJV). He can be relied upon never to change, never to let us down.

And he looks to his people to live similarly, with an uprightness, a moral integrity, a reliability that shows. 'A righteous man who walks in his integrity—blessed are his sons after him!' is how the Book of Proverbs sums it up (Prov 20.7). But it is never easy.

I think of the prisoner released from prison who makes up his mind that he has had enough of the life of crime and punishment. He declares his intention to 'go straight'. He usually means it when he is talking to the prison governor or chaplain, and they congratulate him (and themselves) that he has learnt his lesson. His words sound less confident when spoken down at the local pub with his old associates and far too frequently he gets drawn back to crime because the weakness that led him there has never been addressed and jobs for ex-prisoners are few and far between. His desire for *zedeq* is praiseworthy. We need to ask ourselves what responsibility we have to help him be more successful in achieving it.

BEING FIRM

Another word is found in our text—the word 'faithfulness'.

Great is thy faithfulness. We recognize the phrase from the opening words of a well-known hymn by T. O. Chisholm:

'Great is thy faithfulness', O God my Father,
There is no shadow of turning with Thee;
Thou changest not, Thy compassions, they fail not;
As Thou hast been, Thou for ever wilt be.

In Hebrew the word for faithfulness is *emuna*. It comes from a root meaning 'to be firm'. The word 'amen' has the same derivation. Jesus used it to introduce important sayings: 'Amen, amen, I say unto you'. And of course we use it to conclude our prayers, as if to add our own 'verily' to confirm that we mean what we have just said.

There is also a verb associated with the word, in the form of 'to treat as firm or reliable' or even 'to say amen to'. And that verb *he'emin* is the common Hebrew verb translated 'to believe'. So faith is a matter of saying amen to something, or to someone; to treat God and his word as reliable and trustworthy. That is what it means to believe—not just to think that something is true, but to pin your hopes on it, to rely on it. To rely on God. No wonder that David liked to describe him as a rock, a sure defence, a stronghold. Because that is precisely what he is: faithful for ever.

SHOWING MERCY

It is a feature of our just and righteous God that he is also rich in mercy. So we have that haunting couplet: 'His mercies never come to an end; they are new every morning.' It carries echoes of an incident in the story of Israel's wanderings in the wilderness of Sinai, when Moses was leading them from Egypt into the promised land. Thirsty and hungry they were sustained with water from out of the rock and with manna.

We know very little about the manna and a number of suggestions have been made. Was it the honeydew which exudes from tamarisk trees every June and falls to the ground? Did it owe its origins to insects like cicadas which are known to produce an edible substance in parts of the Sinai peninsula? We frankly do not know. All we are told is that the manna was whitish, with a taste like honey, and appeared in plentiful supply morning by morning. Just like God's mercies! The Book of Exodus adds the further information that it would not keep overnight. It had to be eaten the same day. A new supply must be gathered every day, except of course the Sabbath, for which special arrangements were made.

Now the word mercy describes an attribute of God. His justice is not unfeeling. Though he can be hard on those who despise and disobey him—and the Old Testament contains more than its fair share of blood-curdling descriptions of God acting in judgement—the Lord's nature is best portrayed in Psalm 103:

> As a father pities his children,
>   so the Lord pities those who fear him.
> For he knows our frame;
>   he remembers that we are dust.

There is a difference between mercy and mercies. The former is an aspect of God's character. The latter are the tell-tale signs of his kindliness which are forever being shown to us, if we have the wit to recognize them. Every day they fall new from heaven. Every day there is something different to enjoy. Not because we particularly deserve it, but just because God is like that. I cannot believe that you have no knowledge of these mercies. You must have known them and experienced them. I would only want to remind you that they are more in number than you can ever imagine.

The apostle Paul picks up the same thought when he writes to the Christians in Rome and appeals to them to live lives totally surrendered to God. If they have experienced God's mercies, he says, let this lead them on to self-surrender and a fully dedicated life of service to the Lord. 'I appeal to you therefore, brethren, *by the mercies of God*, to present your bodies as a living sacrifice, holy and acceptable to God, which is your spiritual worship' (Rom 12.1). Have God's mercies led you as far as that moment of surrender to him?

UNCHANGING LOVE

There is another word in our text that we dare not ignore. It is one of the most important words in the Hebrew of the Old Testament. The word is *hesed*, translated variously as loving-kindness, loyalty, steadfast love. It is as much a requirement in human beings as it is a characteristic of God. It is not indiscriminate love, but rather loyalty to a covenant and to those who are in a relationship with you—as we are with God. He shows his *hesed* by keeping his promises and staying faithful and true to us his people, whom he has chosen and called. We need to show our *hesed* to him and to each other by keeping our part of the relationship in obedience and devotion.

We scarcely need to be reminded how much we fail, but God never fails. 'The *hesed* of the Lord never ceases.' His part of the bargain is absolutely watertight. And that is why he can call upon us to aim for, if not always to achieve, similar devotion to the covenant. 'What does the Lord require of you', asks the prophet Micah, 'but to do justice, and to love *hesed*, and to walk humbly with your God?' (Micah 6.8).

Hosea was the great exponent of *hesed*. He learnt it from his own experiences in marriage. The woman he loved deserted him and became a common prostitute but he could not give her up and he went out and did everything he could to woo her back to himself. Then he thought: If I do this for the wife I love, how much more does the God of Israel show *hesed* to his covenant people even though they have persistently rejected him and defiled themselves before the world! And God taught Hosea that God's love too was steadfast, unchanging, never ceasing.

Here then are four great words—righteousness, faithfulness, mercy and love. Together they add up to give us the finest description we could ask for of our God and Father, whom we can see and meet in the person of his Son, Jesus Christ. Four words then, and the greatest of these is love. Hear the text again from Lamentations chapter 3: 'The steadfast love of the Lord never ceases, his mercies never come to an end; they are new every morning; great is thy faithfulness.'

21
NO BACK GATES

Hate evil and love good, and establish justice in the gate.

AMOS 5.15

It has taken me a long time to realize that the people of the Old Testament were not in the habit of having back doors to their houses or back gates to their cities. It was a matter of security. Archaeology confirms this. The remains of Megiddo, for instance, give evidence of strong walls all around the city but only one huge gateway, impressively fortified and protected. There was only one way in and one way out.

So at night the people could close the gates until the morning and that was that. If you arrived too late you had to camp outside, and if you were slow to leave you were penned inside for the night—unless you knew someone who lived by the walls and could let you down from a window. Rahab of Jericho did that for the two spies, you may remember (Josh 2.15), and much later Saul of Tarsus was to escape from trouble in Damascus by the same route (Acts 9.25).

Inside the fortifications there was not a great deal of space. The homes of the inhabitants crammed every corner. So every morning there was the great exodus, as the peasant population escaped to their fields to work in them until it was time to return as the sun went down. That is why the Hebrews invoked the blessing of God 'in your going out and in your coming in', rather than the other way round. Everyone went out by the main gate. There was no back way.

OUTSIDE THE GATE

Overcrowding being what it was there was no room for a central

100

meeting-place. Hebrew towns had no market-square. Instead everything happened just outside the gate. The traders plied their wares, the greybeards gossiped, the elders sat in council and disputes were settled. It was the place where you could be quite sure of catching someone you wanted to meet. It was here that Boaz sorted out the problem of what he was to do about Ruth and her next of kin who had prior rights to her property. You can read about it in Ruth chapter 4;

> Boaz went up to the gate and sat down there; and behold, the next of kin, of whom Boaz had spoken, came by. So Boaz said, 'Turn aside, friend; sit down here'; and he turned aside and sat down. And he took ten men of the elders of the city, and said, 'Sit down here'; so they sat down. Then he said to the next of kin . . .

There was clearly a problem here over the rights of redemption which Boaz needed to sort out if he was going to be able to marry Ruth. It was solved by an *ad hoc* court of ten elders (presumably any ten would have done) before whom Boaz and Ruth's kinsman could publicly pose the problem. There was also an engaging description of the custom whereby transactions were confirmed. It involved taking off one's sandal and handing it to the other person—a rather picturesque way of shaking hands on it.

STANDING IN THE GATE

Notice also how Boaz called on the next of kin and the ten elders to sit down with him in the gate, a sure sign that work in the fields was going to have to be put off until the problem was resolved. To have the right to sit in the gate, in the assembly of the elders, was the Hebrew citizen's great privilege. Even greater was the right to stand in the gate, for you had to stand up to speak and win a hearing. Hence the psalmist says that 'the wicked shall not be able to stand in the judgement, nor sinners in the congregation of the righteous' (Psalm 1.5). They had no case to put; they were condemned already.

Equally it was important that the unprotected should have someone with full citizen rights who would be able to present their case and speak up for them. The widow and the fatherless were particularly vulnerable, as also was the stranger within the gates, the resident alien in modern parlance. They had no family head to represent them and it was an act of great virtue and generosity (and justice, we might add) when someone with standing spoke up on their behalf. On the other hand, a man who was blessed with many children to succeed him and to continue his influence in the community could be described in Psalm 127 as 'Happy is the man who has his quiver full of them! He shall not be put to shame when he speaks with his enemies in the gate.'

INJUSTICE IN THE GATE

With all this background to the Old Testament scenario, it can easily be seen how injustice could have crept in. There were no paid judges, no written body of laws or constitution to which the aggrieved could appeal. Everything depended on the fair-mindedness and integrity of the citizen body. For justice was the preserve of the people. It was rather like our jury system without the presiding judge or expert legal opinion. The potential for error was considerable, the likelihood of partiality was wide open to bribery and other inducements.

So Amos writes (5.12): 'For I know how many are your transgressions, and how great are your sins—you who afflict the righteous, who take a bribe, and turn aside the needy in the gate.' Judges and juries, beware! But most disputes and grievances today are not settled by the courts. The cost is prohibitive in any case. Our problem-solvers are to be found in the corridors of Whitehall, County Hall and our Town and City Halls. Our judges are to be found among the vast army of bureaucrats (I do not use the word pejoratively) who receive complaints, interpret regulations, deal with the public and answer a mountain of letters and enquiries. These are the ones who have the power to turn the needy aside or to see that they are fairly treated, to ensure that justice is done or to keep people waiting in endless uncertainty. They are clerks and minor officials who draw only modest salaries themselves but on whose efficiency and fair-mindedness major sections of our community are dependent. You only have to travel a short distance from our British shores to find countries which have no high traditions for their Civil Service to live up to and where a banknote passed across a counter is the only way to ensure a hearing, let alone justice. And what kind of justice is it that needs to be bought?

JUSTICE AT LAST

There is a saying in the Book of Proverbs, 'He who justifies the wicked and he who condemns the righteous are both alike an abomination to the Lord' (Prov 17.15). It sounds so obvious that one wonders why it was necessary even to mention it. But as usual there is more to the proverb than meets the eye. In Hebrew the words 'wicked' and 'righteous' need not in certain contexts refer to a person's moral character. Instead—and this is particularly true in matters of justice—they become technical terms for the person who is in the right (the righteous) and the person who is in the wrong (the wicked or the guilty). In all other respects their characters may be impeccable, or the reverse. But in the dispute under consideration one is innocent and the other is in the wrong.

The task of judges, whether they are specialists in administering justice, or the disputants' fellow-citizens trying to sort out a quarrel, is to justify (i.e. find in favour of) the person in the right, and to condemn the person in the wrong. As Deuteronomy 25.1 puts it: 'If there be a controversy between men, and they come unto judgement, that the judges may judge them; then they shall justify the righteous and condemn the wicked' (AV). The person who has done nothing wrong cries out to be justified—declared publicly to be what he is: innocent, guiltless. And the judge's job is to do that without being swayed by outside pressure.

103

This talk of the justification of the righteous leads us naturally on to the New Testament where in his letter to the Romans Paul writes of the one who justifies the ungodly (Rom 4.5). This is an astonishing enlargement of what the Old Testament has been insisting upon; indeed it almost turns it on its head. But the criterion of judgement has changed through the life, death and resurrection of Jesus Christ. He has died for sinners, not for the righteous. 'God shows his love for us in that while we were yet sinners Christ died for us' (Rom 5.8). And as a result of his sacrificial death, sinners may be given the verdict, declared to be innocent before God's judgement seat—not because they are no longer sinners but by reason of their reliance upon the God who in Christ justifies the ungodly.

We have come a long way from Megiddo and its main gate, where people met and justice was administered for all who went out and came back in. The cross of Christ is like that for the Christian. It is the place of God's justice, the only one available.

> There was no other good enough to pay the price of sin:
> He only could unlock the gate of Heaven and let us in.

There are no back gates in the matter of God's justice and our sin.

22
LIVING IN LUXURY

*Woe to those who are at ease in Zion . . . who lie upon beds of ivory,
and stretch themselves upon their couches . . . who sing idle songs to the
sound of the harp . . . who drink wine in bowls, and anoint themselves
with the finest oils.*

AMOS 6.1–6

Not long ago the newspapers were full of pictures and comment
about the man with the nation's largest salary. His name is not
particularly memorable but the salary figure of eighteen million
pounds made everyone throw up their hands in horror. In one
year, too. How could it have happened? How could a man's
work be worth all that amount?

The horror was compounded by the discovery that his
paymaster was a bank—a body that has conventionally been
regarded as the epitome of caution and probity. Whatever was a
major bank doing to pay out such a vast sum to one of its
employees? Then we discovered he was not actually an
employee but a man with a good idea who was underwritten by
the bank to test out the market for direct sale insurance. His pay
was related to his success in this new field, on a kind of
commission basis. And, as one of the cheaper papers summed it
up: 'Boy, was he successful!'

I have no doubt that the directors of the bank were kicking
themselves that they had agreed a contract of such generous
terms, but clearly they must have made a very handsome profit
themselves, so they were smiling. The multi-millionaire at the
centre of the storm was not smiling however. He seemed rather
embarrassed and it was easy to see why.

How do you judge a person's worth in monetary terms? Was
he in that one year worth 1,500 clergy, or 200 Cabinet
Ministers? Think how many coal-mines he could have kept
open. But the real question came over differentials: how well

105

was his work-force being rewarded? Where they being tied down to a statutory 2 per cent increase in their salaries, as the rest of us were being told to do?

The word 'obscene' came out in many a comment in the press and from the television screen. They wouldn't have minded if it was won on the pools or in the national lottery. It was the thought that a man was being paid so exorbitantly for work which you or I might have done—*if* we had had the idea, and negotiated the contract, and made it an outstanding success as well. In the end the obscenity element was watered down in the grudging recognition that the man had worked hard for his inflated reward, and the odium turned instead upon the capitalist system which produces such inequalities.

What would the prophet Amos have said in the *Tekoa Times*, if they had given him a column? He was without doubt on the side of the poor. He would see red if he so much as heard a whisper about an oppressive landlord, an unreasonable employer or a partial judge. But he stopped short of attacking wealth for its own sake. Maybe because he was a businessman in a minor way, making regular journeys to Bethel to sell the shearings of his sheep. What he could not abide, however, was the way the wealthy flaunted their riches in enjoying a life of extravagant luxury. That was where his target was drawn.

IDLENESS

'Woe to those who are at ease in Zion . . . who lie upon beds of ivory and stretch themselves upon their couches.' This was anathema to the hard-working, desert-dwelling prophet of Tekoa, who was used to sleeping on the ground and under the stars. What right had these men to idle away their time in their splendid houses, lolling around on couches inlaid with costly ivory and doing nothing whatsoever to improve the lot of anyone but themselves? What kind of stewardship of wealth was this, and what did it do to the vast majority of their fellow-citizens who slaved away to eke out a modest living to keep their families in the basic essentials of life? The differential in wealth was grossly unjust, but the differential in attitude was the real obscenity. And what he regarded as the effete custom of reclining at table instead of sitting upright was just another sign of the decadence which Amos was quick to condemn.

We must not put words into the prophet's mouth but it looks as if his condemnation today would be more of the insidious dangers of inherited wealth, or of being married to wealth, than of actually acquiring it by honest work. If so, he would have much to criticize in our society, where the families of the successful and the inheritors of large fortunes all too frequently provide endless material for the gossip columns, which by turns admire them and rend them to pieces.

GREED

The prophets of the Old Testament draw a discreet veil over the sexual escapades of the well-to-do, though occasionally the veil slips and we see that in this regard they were not all that different from the pampered of our own day. But gluttony was a more obvious vice. After all, it was the peasant and servant class who did the cooking and waiting at table, so they would have known all too well. And like the prodigal son in the far country they would have been glad to eat the leftovers from those piggish feasts. Woe, then, to those who 'eat lambs from the flock and calves from the midst of the stall'.

You can almost hear the disgust as the shepherd condemns those who snatch away the young of the flock to roast them for the table instead of letting them grow to maturity to serve the ewes and to produce young, to clothe people with their wool and then, and only then, to feed a family in a mutton stew. And if Amos raised a query about a dinner of lamb or veal, I wonder what he would make of some of the exotic menus with which we are served up at City dinners or when we are on holiday in France! Gluttony is not only the sin of eating too much. It also includes the sin of eating too well.

FRIVOLITY

The accompaniment of feasting was always music and merry-making, and so those two came under the prophet's lash: 'Woe to those who sing idle songs to the sound of the harp, and like David invent for themselves instruments of music.' At this stage most of us will bridle. What is wrong, we ask, with a little song and dance? And the answer must be that nothing is wrong with it at all. Amos probably twanged a harp or lyre with the best of them at the end of a working day. It was the context that evoked the condemnation. This was the singing and playing of men and women who had not a care in the world, but who ought to have had! They imagined they were 'the notable men of the first of the nations' (verse 1), but in fact they were going to have to give account of their stewardship to God. They felt no pangs of conscience about the ruin of Joseph (verse 6), but in fact their nation was on the brink of collapse, both morally and politically. Amos was aware of it. Others were aware of it. But the idle rich thought nothing of it, only of their selfish passing pleasures. That was what was so galling about their frivolous melody-making and their casual improvisations. They would still be listening to *Top of the Pops* on the eve of Armageddon, is what Amos was trying to say.

EXTRAVAGANCE

The final thrust comes in verse 6. 'Woe to those who drink wine in bowls, and anoint themselves with the finest oils.' One commentator suggests that the bowls referred to were sacrificial bowls, which it was not permissible to drink from; in that case this would be a form of sacrilege. But more likely it was a reference to those who were not content to drink their wine from a goblet but who greedily quaffed it from a bowl. We would say, straight from the decanter. Alongside that, which was surely a guarantee of speedy intoxication if not a sign of advanced alcoholism, was the anointing with the finest scented oils.

A generation ago we would have been hard put to it to find a modern parallel for this. In those days there were no such things as cosmetics for men. But now, thanks to a campaign of media manipulation on the part of the manufacturers, there are almost as many bottles of unguents on a man's dressing-table as on his wife's. After-shave, ante-shave, eau-de-Cologne, hair oil, deodorant, shampoos of various descriptions, talc, it's all there for the man of the house to anoint himself with.

It is of course the acme of vanity. Rarely can it be defended on medicinal grounds, though occasionally a touch of fragrance is one way of covering up one's more anti-social features! Usually people do it just because they like themselves, they like their bodies, they want to make them attractive to the opposite sex. It is a self-centred form of personal preening. And Amos treated it with the contempt it probably deserved.

Yet today in Western society, it is almost normal to use these so-called 'beauty aids'. What we need to learn from Amos is how our 'normal' behaviour is viewed by those on the other side, or from another culture. Amos, the shepherd-farmer from Tekoa, represents the Palestinian or Kurdish refugee, the dweller in London's cardboard city or Saigon's shanty town. How do they assess our wastefulness, our greediness, our self-indulgence, our extravagant (by their standards) life-style? To them a middle-class Western Christian's way of life could well provoke a similar disgust and contempt to that which the idle pampered rich of Samaria stirred up in this old prophet of the Lord.

So forget the eighteen million man whom we look upon with a blend of envy and amazement. It is what the poor of this world think of *us* that matters. And that should make us hang our heads, and think very hard about the way we live and the message this gives out.

23
SHEPHERDS OR BUTCHERS

As for me, I am filled with power, with the Spirit of the Lord, and with justice and might.

MICAH 3.8

It has often been said that a country gets the government it deserves. A weak democracy falls easy prey to tyranny and voters whose choice is controlled by pure self-interest soon find themselves saddled with an administration they do not care for at all.

Much the same can be said of the Church, for there always seems to be a marked correlation between the leaders and the led. Fractious Christians give rise to squabbling Churches, but on the other hand godly pastors produce the fruit of a mature and Spirit-filled laity.

The prophet Micah preached his sermons over the course of three very difficult reigns. Jotham was a good king and the sixteen years he ruled over Judah were given high marks by the Old Testament historians. 'Jotham became mighty, because he ordered his ways before the Lord his God' (2 Chron 27.6). Next came Ahaz, but he did not do what was right in the eyes of the Lord and he got a very definite thumbs down. Finally there was Hezekiah and he reversed the pattern set by his father Ahaz and won the chronicler's accolade. He did what was good and right and fruitful before the Lord his God. 'And every work that he undertook in the service of the house of God and in accordance with the law and the commandments, seeking his God, he did with all his heart, and prospered' (2 Chron 31.21). You cannot find a better epitaph than that.

Nevertheless, Micah found much to criticize and I don't suppose it was all in Ahaz's reign. Chapter 3 of his little book of prophecies points the finger at three groups of people whose wrongdoing was leading the people astray. They were the rulers (verse 1), the prophets (verse 5) and the priests (verse 11).

Micah longed to see his nation as a just society, and he laid the blame for failure fairly and squarely on the shoulders of the nation's leadership. Listen to this:

> Hear, you heads of Jacob and rulers of the house of Israel! Is it not for you to know justice?—you who hate the good and love the evil, who tear the skin from off my people, and their flesh from off their bones; who eat the flesh of my people, and flay their skin from off them, and break their bones in pieces, and chop them up like meat in a kettle, like flesh in a cauldron.
>
> (Micah 3.1–3)

Strong words. And what a vivid metaphor! The rulers were carving up the people instead of caring for them. Making a casserole out of them when they should have been turning them into citizens who were proud to be people of Judah and servants of the living God. The Lord, said Micah, wanted his people to be ruled by shepherds, not by butchers.

The prophets were little better—presumably with the exception of Micah himself as well as Amos, Hosea and Isaiah, his contemporaries. They are accused of doing and saying anything for the sake of a meal-ticket. They cry 'Peace', when they have something to eat, and declare war against the man who puts nothing into their mouths (verse 5). Everything depends on the favours and the fees they receive. I suppose this does have a modern-day parallel. The Christian minister has a natural desire to be well-liked and popular with his people, and when his congregation pays his salary and virtually employs him it must be very difficult for him to maintain his integrity and speak God's word however challenging it may be. In Micah's day the priests too were dominated by money: 'its priests teach for hire, its prophets divine for money' (verse 11). How easily can God's servants be silenced or corrupted by the prospect of unaccustomed wealth. No wonder St Paul's advice to the young Timothy contained that memorable phrase: 'godliness with contentment is great gain' (1 Tim 6.6). They don't often go together.

111

THE SILENCE OF GOD

The rulers, the priests and the prophets are given three final warnings, each more terrifying than the last, in order to bring them to their senses. God's warnings are signals of his love, not just prophecies of doom. They are there to help us to repent and to change our ways. The first is God's silence. 'They will cry to the Lord, but he will not answer them' (verse 4). People who pray (and 90 per cent of people do) often ask why their prayers are not always answered. It may be that God is keeping them waiting to test their sincerity. It may be that the answer is to be 'No' because that is what is for the best. It may be that he is saying 'Not yet'. But there are certainly occasions when the psalmist's words are coming true: 'If I regard iniquity in my heart, the Lord will not hear me' (Psalm 66.18). The fault is not in the Lord, nor in the prayer, but in the heart of the one who is doing the praying. Sometimes God is silent. Beware.

THE DARKNESS OF GOD

Even worse than silence is the darkness of God. 'Therefore it shall be night to you, without vision, and darkness to you, without divination' (verse 6). Just as there are times when God withdraws his voice, so there are times when he withdraws his light. Good Friday was one such day, when there was darkness over the land until the ninth hour. The darkness however is usually symbolical and often spiritual. Christian mystics write about the long dark night of the soul, when vision goes, the sense of God's presence is removed and nothing appears to make sense any more. It is all you can do to hold on to your little grain of faith. It can be a very unnerving experience even for a mature Christian leader to face. But in Micah's day the prophets wished it on themselves and had to bear the ensuing shame and disgrace. Again beware.

THE ABSENCE OF GOD

In the last verse of the chapter comes the final tragedy. 'Because of you Zion shall be ploughed as a field; Jerusalem shall become a heap of ruins, and the mountain of the house a wooded height.' This spells the end of the holy city, the destruction of the temple and the final departure of God from his dwelling-place. Everything worthwhile has come to an end. The glory has departed. On the temple doors hangs a notice saying 'Gone away'.

Now, don't be alarmed. This is a warning, not a reality. We may *feel* that God has abandoned us; we may think we deserve to be deserted; we may wonder what there is about us to keep him taking any notice of us at all. But the simple fact is that he has said 'I will never leave you nor forsake you'. That's in the Old Testament. And the Lord Jesus' last words were 'Lo, I am with you always to the end of time'. That's in the New Testament. So there is no biblical warranty for God ever being absent, only warnings. And the awful possibility of feeling bereft.

FILLED WITH POWER

Into this appalling chapter of failings and warnings, where prophets, priests and kings are all found wanting, come the words of the prophet Micah. 'But as for me, I am filled with power, with the Spirit of the Lord, and with justice and might' (verse 8). Only a man of God can speak with that kind of conviction. And if he was going to declare to Jacob his transgression and to Israel his sin, he needed God's strength in full measure. But the Spirit of the Lord comes not only with power and might, but also with justice. Put it the other way round and you can say that where there is no justice, there is no Spirit of the Lord.

Today we live in an age of the Spirit, when the Holy Spirit is given more prominence than he has received at many other times in the history of the Christian Church. Yet the influence of the Spirit on people's lives is thought of in terms of gifts, like

113

healing and tongues and prophecy, or of power evangelism or of uplifting worship. Rarely, if ever, is he associated with justice, with righteous conduct, with responsible leadership, with fair dealings. Have we, I wonder, got things wrong?

24
WHO CAN STAND?

You have wearied the Lord with your words . . . by asking, 'Where is the God of justice?'

MALACHI 2.17

It was not long ago that the British people were reeling at the shock of a toddler's death. The story of Jamie Bulger's murder at the hands of a pair of children read like a nightmare for every parent in the land. Where had we gone wrong? How could children behave like that? Was there a deep-seated sickness in our society that we needed to address? Who was to blame? The parents? The incidence of broken homes? Video nasties? The Church for failing to teach the moral code? Not for a long time have so many questions been asked by a people wrestling with their own sense of guilt.

The trial of the two boys was equally harrowing, not least for the incessant stream of witnesses who were called. They had seen Jamie being lured away from the shopping precinct where his mother was buying groceries, had noticed his reluctant dawdle with the two ten-year-olds, had seen his tears and heard his crying, and had done nothing to interfere with his progress towards the railway line where eventually his mangled body was found. I lost count of the number of those who gave evidence but it must have been about forty people, all of them eye-witnesses of Jamie's last walk.

Then when it was all over and the two had been found guilty and sentenced, there were the interviews with members of the Bulger family. One cannot blame them for the bitterness they felt but I was glad to see that some of them had found help and consolation from their parish priest. Not all however. One relative was quoted as saying he had no time for a God who had allowed Jamie to die the way he did. Allowed it? Why, he had sent forty people to stop it and none of them had done so! You can't really blame God for everything that happens, when human beings fail to play their part in averting tragedy or in caring for one another the way they should.

BLAMING GOD

Blaming God is invariably the last resort for angry and bewildered people. He must be quite used to it by now. Indeed, the cross exemplifies the way in which God in Christ absorbed so much of the world's hatred and bitterness and derision. And he continues to do so.

So our text is not confined to Old Testament times, with people complaining and asking 'Where is the God of justice?' And let us be fair. There are many occasions when our persistent failure to make sense of life, and the feeling of being hard done by, builds up such a sense of frustration with God that we too batter the gates of heaven and cry out 'What are you doing, God? Don't you care at all? Don't you see what's happening to me? Do something, Lord.'

I can quite easily believe that God waits until we get into that state to see how serious we are. True prayer, persistent, importunate prayer, comes out of that sort of despairing cry. But if we are desperate for justice, we have to meet it on God's terms.

HE IS COMING

The response put into the mouth of God by the prophet Malachi is to say: 'Yes, the Lord whom you seek will suddenly come to his temple.' He *is* going to intervene. He is coming. 'But who can endure the day of his coming, and who can stand when he appears?' The unpalatable fact is that God is not to be called in to be a fairy godmother. If he comes and when he comes, he will come as himself. An uncomfortable God. A God who is more demanding in his holiness than ever we thought. A God of justice indeed.

We are told that his first task will be to purify the sons of Levi, the leaders of the Church, the priesthood. Malachi uses the simile of the silver refiner to illustrate his point. It is a striking and moving picture. For the purifying process takes place under great heat which causes the mixed contents of the refiner's cauldron to bubble and boil, as the lead oxide separates from the pure silver. The dross then rises to the surface and at a certain temperature becomes translucent so that the silver becomes like a mirror. The refiner sits by his cauldron and keeps looking in until the process is complete and he can see his face mirrored in the now purified metal. God refines his people, often through the fires of testing, until he can see his own image reflected in us. Then we shall be pure and more ready to serve him acceptably and, as Malachi puts it, 'Then the offering of Judah and Jerusalem will be pleasing to the Lord as in the days of old'.

A SWIFT WITNESS

As if that was not enough, the prophet then turns his attention from the clergy, the sons of Levi, to the man in the street. 'I will draw near to you for judgement' (the word is the same as the 'justice' for which they have been crying out). 'I will be a swift witness against the sorcerers, against the adulterers, against those who swear falsely, against those who oppress the hireling in his wages, the widow and the orphan, against those who thrust aside the sojourner, and do not fear me, says the Lord of hosts' (Mal 3.5).

What a collection of wrongdoers comes in for condemnation! Perjurers, adulterers and mediums are lumped together with bad employers and those who deny justice to immigrant workers and refugees. Only two of these five sins are specifically condemned in the Ten Commandments, though the sorcerers could well come under the ban on 'other gods before me'. And the commandments do bear witness to a special concern for the stranger that is within the gates. But the likelihood is that these five sins covered some of the major failings of Malachi's hearers, and we are not immune to them today. The morality of the family man is no less important than the ethics of the businessman. Personal dishonesty is on a par with bureaucratic bias. Exploitation of the weak and the defenceless is anathema to the God of justice. And as for preoccupation with the occult, with horoscopes and tarot cards and all the mischievous paraphernalia of latter-day sorcery, they come first in the list of things that qualify for divine judgement. They represent turning one's back on the God who has made himself known, who is light and in whom is no darkness at all.

Verse 6 sums it up. 'I, the Lord, do not change, and you have not ceased to be children of Jacob' (REB). You are deceivers as your forefather Jacob was a deceiver, doing his brother out of his birthright. You are schemers, as your forefather Jacob was a schemer, feathering your own nest at the expense of others. And you are complainers, as your forefather Jacob complained, when he was a victim of the same sharp practice as he had meted out to his father Isaac and his brother Esau. His very name, Jacob, meant a 'heel', and that is precisely what he was and what you, sons of Jacob, have become.

NOW REPENT

So God says 'Return to me and I will return to you'. Repentance is never a one-way street. The prodigal son goes to ask his father's forgiveness and finds his father running out to meet him and to welcome him home. Our embarrassed movements towards God are always met by his generous and loving gestures of acceptance. But the repentance must be more than skin deep. It must be genuine.

Malachi now becomes severely practical, throwing in a play on words for good measure. 'You say, "How shall we return?" Will man rob God? Yet you are robbing me. But you say, "How are we robbing thee?" In your tithes and offerings.' The word for 'rob' consists in Hebrew of the same three letters as the name Jacob, only in a different order. It is not an accident. Are you, he asks, trying to do a Jacob on God? Deceiving him? Supplanting him? And before you say 'No, of course not', just ask yourselves whether you are paying your dues to God: your tithes and your offerings.

It was not the first time in human history nor will it be the last when genuineness in religion is measured by the practical litmus test of what we give to God's work. The tithes were the proportionate gifts relating to income and personal prosperity. The offerings were the voluntary gifts added over and above those that were strictly necessary. The tithes were obligatory, the offerings optional. But in both God was being short-changed.

And then they had the nerve to say 'Where is the God of justice?' No wonder Malachi spluttered with rage at them. For justice is more than getting the wrongs done against you put right. It also shows up the wrongs you do, that you may not even be aware of, and calls upon you to live more righteously before God and your fellow men and women. Make no mistake, none of us can escape the justice of God.